Ask the Organizer

**Answers to Organizing and Productivity
Questions about Your Home, Office, and Life**

Sandra Lane, CPO®

Table of Contents

Introduction

Overflowing closets, overbooked schedules and an overextended life is the norm for many people today. Oftentimes, we struggle through and adapt to the chaos when all we may need is some guidance. A little hand-holding. A fresh set of eyes looking at a situation or space.

Hello! My name is Sandra Lane. I am your friendly neighborhood professional organizer. I have been in the organizing industry since 2010. I have had the pleasure of working with hundreds of clients through their organizing and time management challenges.

When I meet someone new who learns about my business, I usually entertain a variety of questions such as, "my daughter can't decide what clothes to take to college" ... or "I know I need a better filing system but don't know how to create it" ... or "what can I do about my kid's stuff in the entryway?" Over the years, I've welcomed the questions and the work because it's so gratifying to help others.

I compiled many of those questions and answers as content for a weekly blog that I wrote for a local community website. I was doing what I could to spread my organizing message. A few years later, I was invited to write a monthly column for our local paper. The content of the column continued to focus on problem-solving and troubleshooting everyday organizing issues.

This book is a collection of those blogs and columns, with many more suggestions added in for good measure, all in a question and answer format. You'll find bonus tips and inspirational quotes designed to support your organizing and productivity endeavors.

I wanted the book to be as reader-friendly as possible. I think you will find the Q & A format allows you to stop and start your reading with ease. The chapters are categorized by areas and issues of the home, office or life so you can search for a specific topic.

Throughout the book, I use the term 'edit' to describe the process of deciding what you want to release or keep. In the organizing industry you may hear the words "purge", "clear out", "let go", "downsize", "reduce" or "eliminate." The meaning is the same — "edit" is my word of choice.

My goal for this book is to provide you with actionable solutions that cover a range of subjects from too many clothes to too little time and everything in between while motivating and supporting you through each step.

You'll see I refer to the **ATO Pinterest board**.

What is that?

On this board, you can view photos which support the written descriptions mentioned in the book.

Two ways to find the ATO Pinterest board:

1. Visit my website, organizationlane.com, and go to the Resources tab.

2. You can also go directly to Pinterest and search for Organization Lane.

Signing up for Pinterest is easy and free, go to pinterest.com.

If you like this book, please don't keep it a secret. I invite you to tell your friends about it and write a review on Amazon. I thank you in advance.

Getting you on the Road to Productivity!

INSIDE YOUR HOME

Nest, crib, cottage, house, manor, palace,
condo, bungalow, trailer, shack, hut, cabin or villa.

No matter how you refer to your home and no matter its size, you can arrange it with improved storage, comfort and function.

*A house is just a place to keep your stuff
while you go out and get more stuff.*

❧ George Carlin ☙

Kitchen

1. What is the best way to organize my spices?

Spice storage can be a challenge depending on the size and layout of your kitchen and the number of spices you have on hand.

Begin your organization project by letting go of any old or outdated spices. Though there may not be an expiration date listed on your favorite herbs or spices, they do lose their flavor and potency after 3–4 years. If you find duplicate containers of spices, consolidate into one container or toss out the oldest one.

Logistically, it would be more convenient to store your spices near the cooking area for easy reach during food preparation but that may not be possible for every kitchen's configuration so here are a variety of possible solutions that could work for you. View them all on my ATO Pinterest board.

> **ATO Pinterest board**: view photos which support the written descriptions mentioned in the book by visiting the website, organizationlane.com, and go to the Resources tab. Or go directly to Pinterest and search for Organization Lane.

- If you are storing spices in a cabinet, a lazy Susan is a great tool which will allow you to see each spice.

- Installing a pull-out shelf to an existing cabinet is a practical option for spices which will make each one visible and accessible. Check with Shelf Genie (www.shelfgenie.com) or a handyman for installation.

- Shelf racks or tiered racks maximize your cabinet space without taking up a large footprint. Their stacking design provides the right storage for small spaces.

- A clever way to store spices in a small kitchen came from a client who used the inside of a pantry door, 3 M hooks, twine, spices in sealed bags and binder clips to keep them in place.

- If you are short on drawer and cabinet space, install a wall mount spice rack on the inside of a pantry door.

- If you have drawer space, lay spice bottles down on their side next to each other. This is how I arranged the spices in my kitchen. And yes, I alphabetized them. I would not want to mistakenly reach for cayenne pepper when I want to use paprika. These two spices look exactly the same in their bottle but would certainly not taste the same. Don't laugh but I've actually had guests in my home take pictures of my spice drawer.

- Add a small decorative shelf to your backsplash to hold spices in jars. Even if they are out in the open, pretty jars can look tidy.

Bonus: If your newly purchased spice does not list an expiration date, use a permanent marker to indicate the date of purchase on the top or bottom of the container. This will be your future cue of when to let it go.

2. Where do you suggest storing large kitchen cooking utensils such as ladles and spatulas?

Ideally, the placement of these large utensils should be in close proximity to where you use them.

First go through your utensils and be sure you need/use everything. How many potato mashers does one household need? In case you're wondering, the answer is one. Here are a few storage ideas that can work in any kitchen:

- Use a decorative container to hold your most frequently used utensils (if you are short on drawer space this is a good option). Place the container near your cook top surface for easy access.

- If you have the drawer space, use drawer inserts or dividers to keep utensils compartmentalized and prevent them from becoming a tangled mess. Organize them by putting similar items together.

- Install hooks onto the side of a cabinet or back splash which will allow you to hang your utensils and still keep them within reach.

3. Help, my refrigerator is a mess!

Don't you hate that mess? It happens. Here is a step by step approach to cleaning out a refrigerator and getting it organized.

1. **Empty everything out** of the refrigerator and place it on your counter.

2. **Throw out old or expired products** in order to make room for fresh items.

3. **Consider storing leftovers in clear containers** so you can easily see what you have and use masking tape to label the pack date.

4. **Wipe out** all flat surfaces in the refrigerator using your preferred cleaning solution. Pull out vegetable drawers and clean with soap and water.

5. **Containerize!!** When you begin returning items to the refrigerator, consider using clear plastic bins to corral smaller, similar items together. This will prevent items from being pushed to the back of the refrigerator and forgotten. Food that does not get eaten in a timely manner is lost money, so these containers are a worthy investment. Items such as string cheese, juice boxes or yogurt cups could neatly fit into a storage container. A lazy Susan can hold condiments such as ketchup, mustard, jams, hot sauce, etc.

6. **Lastly, edit the front of your refrigerator** of any unnecessary magnets, pictures and outdated notes and give it a wipe down.

4. I have a small kitchen, in my apartment, with limited cabinet space and I love to cook. Any ideas for storage of my pots and pans? Right now, they are in my hall closet.

Even small kitchens can serve the most devoted cook.

Secure professional installation and go vertical! Using a pot rack or hooks suspended from a ceiling can be an optimal solution for small spaces.

If you have the floor space, purchase a free-standing island equipped with storage. They come in a variety of sizes. If you add wheels to the piece, you can roll it out of the way when it's not needed. See this on the ATO Pinterest board.

5. We unpacked from our move haphazardly and my kitchen has no organization to it. I'm not sure what should go where. Please help!!

Kitchens are one of the hardest spaces to unpack because of the many different items that belong in this space and the various storage options available to you. No matter what size kitchen you have, you can set up an organized space that creates a workflow to meet your needs. Keep these tips in mind:

1. **Empty out.** Pull out all items from each cabinet and drawer. Wipe down the surfaces inside and out. Set everything on your counter for a closer look.

2. **Make decisions.** If you did not make downsizing decisions before you moved, now is the time. Unused or duplicate items take up important real estate. Throw away broken items and donate unused items to charity.

3. **Store items according to your workflow.** Group items related to a specific task and place them near your designated work area. Some examples are:

   - Designate a cabinet near your coffee maker as a coffee zone. Use this cabinet to hold all coffee essentials, such as ground coffee, cups, sugar bowl, etc.

   - Place trash bags near the trashcan.

   - Store pots, pans and potholders near the stove.

   - Keep kitchen towels near the sink.

   - Place spices near your food prep area.

   - In your designated baking cabinet place measuring cups, cupcake liners, decorative sprinkles, cake mixes, measuring spoons, mixing bowls etc.

   - Have sandwich bags, plastic wrap, and food storage containers near your sandwich-making area.

4. **Clear your counter.** A kitchen counter provides a limited amount of space that can get cluttered quickly. Consider what really needs to live on your counter and remember that less stuff means more room to prep meals!

6

More tips to keep in mind:

- Keep frequently used items where it is easier to reach them and less used items tucked in the back of a cabinet.

- Improve the visibility of items in a deep cabinet by using a lazy Susan, shelf risers or pull out gliding shelves.

- Remove dry goods (cereal, nuts, rice) from their bags or boxes and store them in airtight clear jars or plastic containers to maintain freshness and keep your space in order. Want to see it? Check out the ATO Pinterest board.

- Save on space by nesting bowls, pans and food storage containers.

- Edit your pantry and refrigerator too. Dispose of all items that are beyond their "use by" date.

- Store less frequently used items elsewhere in the house. (i.e. roasting pan used for Thanksgiving dinner only; seasonal items such as grilling and picnic supplies).

- Place kids dishes and cups where they can reach them easily so they may help set the table.

6. I need a better system to store and manage the paper that surrounds my kids' school and sports activities. It's taking up space on my kitchen counter and that does not work for me. Any ideas?

The kitchen is a common place for these items to collect. Utilizing a wall or the inside of a kitchen cabinet door could be your answer. You can secure a cork or white board for messages, a wall mount file rack to store papers and a calendar. This arrangement will give you accessibility, visibility and help you reclaim some counter space.

Another option is to use a portable file box to store papers. This will provide you with the ability to tuck the box away when it's not in use, accessibility of papers and mobility. You can see this on the ATO Pinterest board.

7. How can I keep my plastic food storage containers in order?

Food storage containers are essential for keeping leftovers, packing lunches and sending food home with guests. How we store them can make life easier when we need to reach for one.

Do a quick edit of your containers to be sure you have lids to match each container. Missing lids fall into the same twilight zone as missing socks in the laundry. Let go of any containers missing their lids.

Use drawer dividers that can expand to fit any size drawer. These dividers will create sections in your drawer where you can store lids in one section and nest the containers in another section. Take a look on the ATO Pinterest board.

> **Bonus:** Food containers without matching lids can be repurposed for use with crafts (paint, beads, stickers, etc.) or as containers to store smaller items in a drawer or cabinet.

8. I have cookbooks taking up space in my kitchen cabinet. I know I need to get rid of some, I'm just not sure how to decide.

Cookbooks can inspire and motivate us to cook. They can also accumulate and go untouched for years.

Review each of the books and take an inventory of what recipes you use and how often. If you are not using them then there is no reason to have them take up real estate in your cabinet. Donate them to your local library.

If you only use a few special recipes in a cookbook, why keep the entire book? Make a copy of the recipe and release the book. Store the recipe in clear sheet protectors and place them in a loose-leaf binder. Create cooking categories for your binders such as crock pot cooking, vegetarian, pastas, meats, etc.

A cookbook is worth keeping if you use multiple recipes in it several times throughout the year.

One final thought: consider where else you can find recipes that will not take up any space at all...the internet!! Thousands of recipes can be found online so there is never a need to bring a new cookbook into your house.

9. Our new house has deep kitchen cabinets. On numerous occasions, I've found old and forgotten items in the back of the cabinets.

It's nice to have the storage of a deep cabinet but it can also create a problem of forgotten items stored in the space.

Pull out shelves will allow you to not only see what you have in the back of the cabinet but also provide easy access. There are custom and DIY designs available that can turn any standard cabinet into one with pull out gliding shelves.

10. I can't find anything in my pantry — how can I keep it organized?

Pantry storage can hold a variety of items and be used by many family members so keeping it organized can be a challenge. Here are my suggestions to get it organized:

- Use labeled clear jars with air-tight lids to store dry goods such as rice, nuts, flour and sugar. These jars create a tidy appearance and keep foods fresher than the original packaging.

- Clear, air-tight cereal containers make it easier to see what needs replenishing.

- You can find what you're looking for when you group similar items together just as you would see in a grocery store, i.e. soups, beans, pasta, snacks, drinks, etc.

- Use baskets/bins to hold a group of smaller items, i.e. snack/ protein bars, popcorn or lunch size treats.

- If you purchase in bulk, keep only a few weeks' worth of product in the pantry and store the rest of your supply elsewhere in the home. Replenish your pantry supply as needed.

- Use shelf risers to improve the visibility of canned goods.

- When you create your shopping list for needed supplies, take time to straighten out any disorder in your pantry.

11. Meal planning is a nightmare for me. What ideas do you have to make it easier?

Life is moving at a fast pace and sitting down to a family meal is a good time to connect, so let's make it happen. Here are a few ideas I share with my clients:

- **Double up.** If you're already making one casserole dish, make another to freeze for a later date. Label the casserole and include the assemble date.

- **Batch cooking.** Set aside a day to make freezer meals for future use. There are various websites to help facilitate a week to a month's worth of meals. You can search for that by using the term 'batch cooking'.

- **Plan for the week.** Choose one day a week to plan the meals for the week. Gather your shopping list, recipes, family schedules, and coupons for the week. Plan each meal based on after-school activities as you may need to make a meal on the go.

> **Bonus:** Save time in the grocery store by writing out your shopping list according to the store's product layout.

- **A salad is easier than you think.** Salad prep can be the most time-consuming part of a meal. My solution is to chop all of the vegetables in advance and store them in an air-tight container (peppers, carrots, onions, cucumbers, but don't add the tomatoes). When it's time to make a salad, grab a few handfuls of pre-washed chopped lettuce (sold in grocery stores) and toss into a bowl, add the pre-cut veggies, some cherry tomatoes and whalah!

- **Fav meal.** Always have ingredients on hand for the family's favorite and fast go-to meals i.e. Taco Tuesday, Spaghetti Wednesday, Pizza Friday. Call it what you like but have it stocked.

- **Collect easy recipes.** Start building up a collection of easy recipes with an online search of '3-5 ingredient' recipes.

- **Outsource it.** If it's in your budget, there are several companies that will shop, suggest meal ideas and deliver right to your door; for example, Blue Apron and Hello Fresh. You can also check out your local grocery store, they may offer shopping, delivery or pickup options as well.

- **Rinse and repeat.** Using a calendar template, fill in all of your meal ideas. When you have created a menu of meals for 2-4 weeks, simply repeat. Remember, the objective is to sit down together and nourish your family.

12. I have unused space in my corner cabinets. Any idea how I can make the most of the space in that area?

Don't relinquish this dead space as it could be very useful, especially if you have a small kitchen.

A skilled carpenter can transform a corner cabinet into a lazy Susan or create custom pull out drawers. This is worth a look — check out my ATO Pinterest board.

13. What do you suggest for freezer organization?

Here's a common scenario — you can't find an item in your freezer and you buy it again. Or an item gets buried in your freezer and never gets used.

With the rising cost of food, a poorly organized freezer can become a waste of money. Here's how to keep up with your freezer inventory and save a few dollars in the long run:

- If you purchase bulk size packages of meats and vegetables, take a few minutes to separate these items into smaller storage bags. Label the bags with the item and purchase date.

- Use labeled plastic bins to store items into categories. Bin labels can include: Meats, Fish, Poultry, Fruits, Vegetables and Treats.

- Use a clip board or note pad attached to the front of your freezer complete with a written inventory of its contents. Make a notation when you remove an item and add it to your shopping list if you're running low.

- If you have a deep freezer, this can really become a black hole for your food. Measure the inside of your freezer for length and width. Shop for plastic containers that will fit side by side on the bottom and allow you to place another layer of bins stacked on top of the bottom bins. Designate each container for a different category of food and use the inventory system mentioned above.

14. Can you help me make my junk drawer look less junky?

Every kitchen needs a junk drawer and keeping it neat is a common challenge.

Here's your step by step guide to getting your junk drawer cleaned out and arranged so it looks less junky and serves you well:

1. Empty the drawer and wipe out the inside.

2. Spread the drawer contents onto a flat surface. Sort similar items together.

3. Toss out dried out pens, markers and anything else that is broken or worn out.

4. If you have items that should not live in this drawer, set those items aside. Deliver these items to the appropriate place in your house after your work on the drawer is complete.

5. Decide what should go back into the drawer. Limit items to what you use regularly and makes the most sense to keep in this space.

6. Purchase small containers to corral similar items together. Containers or drawer inserts will also help keep items from rolling around in a drawer every time someone opens and closes it.

> **Bonus:** Cardboard jewelry boxes (lids and bottoms) or other small boxes of various sizes can be repurposed to serve as practical containers to hold items.

7. Lay down a rubber drawer liner first as this will prevent the containers from shifting.

8. If your junk drawer begins to show signs of disorder, take a few minutes and perform a quick maintenance visit. This is a 5-minute visit to (1) pull out items that have migrated to the drawer that do not belong, (2) reorganize items so they are in the correct container, and (3) toss out anything that is broken.

15. We are an active family so we have lots of water bottles. What suggestions do you have for storage?

First, a quick edit. Be sure the bottles you are storing are being used. We all gravitate towards our favorites. Let go of the ones you don't use. Check to make sure each bottle you keep has a matching lid.

Storage options:

- A deep drawer allows you to lay the bottles down so every bottle is visible. A small container within the drawer can hold the lids.

- Stackable water bottle racks are available online. They are similar to a wine rack and can fit into a cabinet or on a shelf. (ATO Pinterest board)

- An over-the-door shoe bag will store 24 bottles!! (ATO Pinterest board)

Clutter: anything that stands between you and the life you want to be living.

&ᴥ Peter Walsh ᴥ

Bath

16. What suggestions do you have for making the most of my small bathroom space?

When it comes to storage options, a small bathroom requires some 'out of the box' ideas since traditional storage options may not fit. Here are a few thoughts and please visit the ATO Pinterest Board to see them:

- Store only your most frequently used items in the bathroom. Stow the rest nearby but not in the bathroom.

- A dainty pedestal sink offers no under cabinet storage. Rather than replace the sink, search the internet for a custom cabinet to surround your pedestal sink.

- Use a clear pocket over-the-door shoe holder (can you tell, I love these!) for storage of small bathroom and hygiene supplies.

- If your budget and home design allow, build recessed storage into a wall.

- Save on space by purchasing small sizes of your favorite health and beauty items.

- Install shelves or a free-standing cabinet on the wall space above the commode.

- Add a shelf over the bathroom door. This can provide useful storage without taking up any floor space.

Happiness is a place between too little and too much.

❧ Finnish proverb ❧

17. My teenager has makeup supplies spread out all over her bathroom and bedroom. She is often late to school because she can't find what she's looking for. How can I help her?

Grooming habits increase overall clutter in the bathroom. Working together, gather all of her beauty items from all locations into one work space and follow these steps:

1. **Edit**. Encourage her to look through everything. Does she <u>use and need</u> all of the products? We can sometimes collect an abundance of makeup because we try it once, don't like it but hang onto it indefinitely. Toss out any old or expired makeup. Due to bacteria buildup, experts suggest replacing makeup products every six months when used regularly and even more frequently for eye makeup.

2. **Placement.** Choose a home base for all of her items. This space should have a mirror, electrical outlet, good lighting, drawers or shelves to hold her supplies. You can use more than one space but keep similar items together. For example, store all nail polishes and related nail care supplies in her bedroom. Hair care products and makeup can be stored in the bathroom. Store items in a hand-held caddy for mobility.

3. **Containerize.** Sort and separate hair accessories, face, nail and dental care items into various containers.

18. We need more towel drying space in our bathroom. Any ideas?

This is a problem in my bathroom too! Here are a few ideas that may help you:

*   Over the door hooks are a quick fix and require no drilling.

*   There are shower curtain rods that come with an attached towel bar providing nearly 6 feet of space for drying towels. You can see this on my ATO Pinterest board.

*   A tension shower rod can be used for more than just a shower curtain. When placed in the right location, it's a quick fix in providing plenty of hanging towel space. (ATO Pinterest board)

19. What suggestions do you have for under-the-sink storage ideas?

Space under a sink is often overlooked or underutilized for storage. Here are some ideas for you:

- The cabinet under a sink can be deep and dark making it difficult to see what is inside. I recommend pull out shelves which can bring everything forward and into the light. (ATO Pinterest board)

- Clear shoebox size bins with lids for storage. Label the bins with the contents and stack on top of each other to utilize that dead air space in your cabinet.

- Tiered racks are available that can fit inside your cabinet and provide shelf space for two levels of items.

- Wire baskets built to hook over the cabinet door can provide extra storage. Find one to fit your cabinet which can hold cleaning supplies, a blow dryer, curling iron or brushes. (ATO Pinterest board)

20. We have 4 kids sharing one bathroom. What ideas do you have to help keep their stuff from blending together?

Yuk! Not fun using a toothbrush or razor that's not yours. Here are a few ideas that will keep items in a shared space from blending together:

Shower/Bath:

- A shower caddy tension rod provides four shelves of storage. The rod wedges into the space between the ceiling and the tub corner. Designate one shelf per person to store their shower essentials.

- Another option: have each person use their hand-held shower caddy, which they can bring to the bathroom.

Towels:

- Set up designated hooks with a decorative initial for each family member to keep towels separate and off the floor.

- Each child can have a designated colored towel.

Drawers:

- If you have the drawer space, designate one drawer per person for their miscellaneous bathroom supplies.

- One drawer can be used for all toothbrushes and toothpaste. Repurpose a utensil tray and label each slot with a name to keep toothbrushes separated. See this and all the ideas here on the ATO Pinterest board.

- A different color toothbrush for each family member is another good cue of who's brush belongs to whom.

21. I have long hair and therefore a lot of hair accessories. How can I keep them organized?

With long hair comes all of the accoutrements to keep it looking nice. Here are my suggestions to keep hair accessories organized:

- Use a plastic caddy with handle to hold hair styling products and tools. You can easily pull out the caddy and keep inventory of what you have or need.

- There are wall mount and over-the-cabinet-door storage baskets for blow dryers and curling irons. Find one that suits your space.

- A jewelry pocket travel organizer can be repurposed to hold your various hair accessories separated and visible. (ATO Pinterest board)

- Small containers or jars in a drawer can separate and store hair clips, pins and bands.

22. How can I create a linen closet worthy of a magazine photo shoot?

Inspiration from magazines are great but it's not just about how it looks; your linen closet should be functional, as well. Here are my thoughts:

- Always begin with an edit of your linens. Do you have mis-matched sheets or incomplete sets? Anything ripped or fraying? How many towels do you really need? Donate your unwanted items to an animal shelter or Goodwill.

- If you are short on space, store out-of-season items on higher shelves or in another closet. When the seasons change, make the switch from winter linens to summer.

- Save the zippered bags your blankets and comforters are sold in and use them to store bulky items when they are not in use. If you do not have the original bag, Ziploc® makes large size storage bags. (ATO Pinterest board) or you may prefer vacuum sealed bags to save on space.

- In order to achieve that pristine look of folded sheets on a shelf, I recommend: 1) Place your fitted sheet and pillow cases within a neatly folded flat sheet. 2) Wrap it up burrito style. This will keep a complete set together. 3) Place on a shelf with the folded side facing outward. 4) Stack sheets of similar sizes together and label the shelf (king, queen, full or twin). You can see the step by step fold on the ATO Pinterest board.

- The appearance and fit of towels on your shelf will depend on how you fold them. Work with the shelf size you have to make it fit. It will look neater if you place the folded side of the towel facing outward.

- Your linen closet may also be a storage area for health and beauty aid supplies. Separate items into categories and store in baskets or clear shoe box size bins and label. For example, you could have the following categories: first aid, nail care, cold and flu care, pet care, etc. See my baskets on the ATO Pinterest board.

- We don't always have the time to carefully put away linens (or our kids/spouse "help" with the laundry) so things may get out of order every now and again. Every 3 months, revisit your linen closet for a little tidying up.

Bedroom & Closets

23. My closet is stuffed to capacity. How can I deal with my clothing clutter?

Statistics show that we wear only 20% of what we have in our closet.[1] That means there is a good chance we have clothes in our closet that are simply taking up space. If you're looking to "unstuff" your closet, then you need to make some decisions.

1. **Make an appointment with your closet.** Depending on the size of your closet, this may take some time and multiple appointments, so be patient with yourself. Mark your calendar and stick to the appointment. Recruit a friend or professional organizer for help and accountability. We can always find something else to do when that appointment comes up on our calendar but when you have a partner to hold you accountable, it's harder to wiggle out of the scheduled time you've planned for this work.

2. **Work in small sections.** Looking at the entire closet all at once can be overwhelming. Pull out a small grouping of clothes from your closet and lay them out on your bed.

3. **Ask yourself some questions.** Look at each piece of clothing and consider the following: Do you love it? Does it flatter your figure? Is it a good color for you? Have you worn it in the last year? If you haven't worn it, why not? Will you ever wear it? Is it still in style? Is it a relevant piece of clothing for the life you live now? You may also need to take some time to try a few things on to check for fit. Don't assume anything fits or it's comfortable. Take the time to try it on and be sure an item makes the cut.

4. **Create 3 piles**. (Donate — Keep — Specialty)

    • **Donate**. If you answered "no" to any of the above questions then place these clothes in a donate bag with no regrets. These clothes served you at one time in your life and now they no longer do. Donate them so they can serve someone else. Choose a charity meaningful to you.

- **Keep**. The next pile you may create will be the items that will go back into the closet. These will be clothes that you love. Clothes that you said "yes" when you answered all the questions above.

  If you have clothes in your keep pile that need mending or cleaning, rather than put them back in your closet take them to your car and plan a drop off to the tailor or dry cleaner.

- **Specialty**. The last pile will consist of specialty items. These will be clothes you said "yes" to but are out of season, less frequently worn, or worn for special occasions only. If you have the space, create an auxiliary storage area for these items. This can be another closet in a spare bedroom, attic, or basement.

Switching clothes from one season to another is your opportunity to review the clothes in your closet before sending them off to your auxiliary storage area. If you did not wear it this past season, why? Your answer may reveal that these items can be donated.

> **Bonus:** Now that you have edited your closet, commit to a *one-in-one-out* **rule** to maintain the quantity of clothes in your space. The rule is simple: when you buy one new item, donate one item.

24. I have a small bedroom in my apartment with little storage space. What suggestion do you have to store out-of-season clothes?

You might find the storage space you need right under your bed.

- If you need to create the space, use bed risers to gain a few inches of height.

- Plastic storage bins can fit under your bed to store bulky items, out-of-season clothes and shoes.

- Old dresser drawers from a flea market can be repurposed as under bed storage by adding wheels under the drawer. Visit my ATO Pinterest board to see this repurposed idea.

25. My purses and handbags are a mess. How can I keep them in some kind of order?

Handbags and clutch purses require their own unique storage space and care.

- In order to have your hand bags sit upright on the shelf and to preserve their original shape, I encourage clients to keep the paper stuffing that comes with the bag. When the bag is not in use, keep it stuffed.

- Handbags are an investment which need extra protection in your closet. You may want to consider dust covers (Amazon). A pillowcase works well too. Be sure to tag or label the dust cover so you know which bag is inside.

- Depending on the size of your closet, there are several storage options for your handbags including: bins, shelf dividers, and S-hooks hanging on a closet rod which can hold bags with handles.

- A free-standing book shelf in your closet makes a great place to store bags. (ATO Pinterest board)

26. I am now a stay at home mom with no intention of going back into the corporate field. I have many high-end business suits that I no longer need. Can you suggest a purposeful donation option?

Kudos to you for making the decision to release a part of your wardrobe and do it with purpose and meaning.

Nationally, you can find an appropriate charity that will accept your business clothes by visiting www.guidestar.org or www.dressforsuccess.org.

Here in the Pittsburgh area we have a few great organizations that specifically assist women in transition to get back on their feet or into the work force including:

- Treasure House Fashions, Pittsburgh PA, www.thfashions.org
- Center for Hope, Ambridge, PA, www.centerforhope.com
- Dress for Success, downtown Pittsburgh, www.dressforsuccess.org
- Other options listed on www.wcspittsburgh.org

27. My nightstand is a cluttered mess; do you have any suggestions?

A nightstand is the last thing you see before you drift off to sleep and the first thing you see when you wake up. Let's make it a pleasant visual instead of one that is distressing.

- Use a night stand with storage. A piece with drawers, open storage, or closed cabinet doors will allow you to tuck items away when they are not in use and keep the top of your night stand clear.

- Edit the current contents of your nightstand. If you find an item that is no longer in regular use or not needed then relocate it, donate it or toss it.

- Use small containers (with or without lids) in your night stand drawer to keep small items in place.

- If you don't have the room for a night stand you can use a bedside or mattress caddy to store a few essentials close to your bed. This caddy stays in place when you slide it in between your box spring and mattress. The pockets hang along the side of your bed, which allow you to store your favorite book, phone and more. (ATO Pinterest board)

Clutter is nothing more than postponed decisions.

&ed; Unknown &es;

---

28. I would like to have a bedroom that I can call my sanctuary. How can I achieve that look?

We should all be striving to create a sanctuary in our sleep space. A restful night of sleep is important for our bodies to recharge and rejuvenate. We owe it to ourselves to create a bedroom that can encourage a peaceful slumber each night and here's how to accomplish it:

- Clutter in a bedroom is a visual distraction. Excess clothes that are spilling out of drawers and closets need a home. Create the hanging or drawer space required by making decisions of what you need, love and use. See question #23 to learn more about organizing your clothes.

- Be selective and limit pictures and mementos to those that make you happy and calm.

- Make your bed!! It's the biggest piece of furniture in your room and when it's not neatly made, the whole room looks disorganized and messy.

- Remove unused or unnecessary pieces of furniture. They may be adding to the feeling of clutter in the room.

- If your bedroom is home to a desk, television or exercise equipment, remove them if possible or use a screen to hide them. These furniture pieces scream *stimulation* and that does not correlate to *rest*.

- Clear your night stand and conceal your essentials and night time reading in a drawer. See question #27 to learn more about night stand organization.

A place for everything and everything in its place.

∂ Old saying, circa early 1600's ∾

Other stuff in your home

29. My entryway is a cluttered mess! How can our family keep this area neat?

The entryway of any home, no matter the size, is a common place for clutter to collect. Mail, backpacks, coats and shoes all end up in this small space.

Everything that may be there now can't stay due to lack of space. The solution begins with a decision of what items you have the space for and then create a place for everything to live. For example, if you find your kid's hockey or lacrosse bags take up too much space in the entryway, the bags will have to be dropped off elsewhere in the house.

Once you've determined how your entryway can function and serve your family, bring in items to facilitate your needs. Some common entryway tools include:

- A bench with a basket placed underneath for shoe collection. Or a bench with a lid for storage of shoes or outerwear accessories.

- Hooks or a coat tree for outerwear and backpacks. You can also find furniture pieces that accomplish these tasks by visiting the ATO Pinterest board.

- A narrow table or cabinet is an ideal surface space for a bowl or basket to store keys, loose change or anything else that may come from emptying coat pockets.

- If you decide incoming mail will land in the entryway, use a small basket to hold it all.

- A container or hooks for umbrellas.

- A mirror can offer you one last look before heading out the door.

30. Every bedroom in my house is occupied but I need to create a small home office area. Any ideas?

An office does not have to be limited to a specific room or a traditional desk.

- You can create a workspace anywhere using a wardrobe closet. Customize the piece by pulling out or adding shelves. Pull up a chair and use your laptop on the main shelf. Lower cabinets can hold a file box and other supplies. On the inside of cabinet doors, mount file holders, a cork or magnet board, and calendar. When your "office" is not in use you can close the doors and keep everything hidden. This repurposed project can be found on the ATO Pinterest board.

- Another option is to empty out a closet and use it for an office space. Add electrical outlets, a desk top, file cabinets, overhead storage and you're open for business. You can see a picture of Organization Lane headquarters, in our converted closet, on the ATO Pinterest board.

31. I tell my husband all the time, the clutter in his den is going to make him sick. What do you think?

Absolutely! Clutter and disorganization in the home or office have been linked to stress, increased anxiety, inadequate sleep, poor eating and exercise habits, and even allergies. If you are unhappy with your environment it will adversely affect your mental and physical health.

However, if you are happy with your surroundings, it can positively impact your mood, energy level and overall attitude.

Here is further documented information to support your intuition:

1) Clutter can cause stress. (University of South Carolina study)[2]

2) It is more difficult to focus when living or working in a cluttered environment. (Trends in Cognitive Sciences)[3]

3) Mental clutter can cause less efficient thinking. (University of Toronto study)[4]

4) Disorganized and messy spaces can lead to unhealthier eating. (Australian-US study)[5]

Time spent organizing and de-cluttering your home or workspace is an investment in your health and well-being. That is time well spent!

OUTSIDE YOUR HOME

Some spaces are hard to organize because they are multi-purpose. A garage and our cars fall into this category. As a result, these spaces can become a cluttered hodgepodge of possessions.

It is possible to bring order, clarity and function to these areas of your life.

The secret to happiness, you see, is not found in seeking more, but in developing the capacity to enjoy less.

ॐ Socrates ॐ

32. We want to have a garage sale — what should we do first?

I'm not going to sugar coat this — a garage/yard sale is a lot of work and can be a disappointment when your earnings do not correlate with the time and effort you spend preparing for the sale.

Having said that, if you and your family are ready to move forward, begin by setting a date for the sale. This date will be your motivating deadline to de-clutter your house in a timely manner.

Use the checklist below to prepare an organized and successful sale:

1. **Set up a staging area.** As you walk through your house searching for items you no longer use or have a need for, set them aside in a designated staging area. This space should accommodate a large amount of goods and remain undisturbed until your sale date.

2. **Advertise.** Two weeks before your sale date, call newspapers or go online to create a classified advertisement announcing your sale. Secure your ad for the week of the sale and be sure to mention the time/date and highlight some of the larger or specialty items you will have for purchase, i.e. furniture, toys or collectibles. Utilize social media sites to spread the word as well.

3. **Make signs.** Use bright colored poster board (at least 11"x17") to make signs with directional arrows leading towards your home or simply list your address. A few days before the sale, post the signs throughout your neighborhood. (Don't forget to take down your signs after the sale is over).

4. **Gather your supplies in advance.** On the day of the sale, you will need: chairs for sitting; tables to display your wares; masking tape or sticky dots and a marker for pricing; a wardrobe rack for any clothing; bins to group similar items together; plastic baggies to group small items; and some start-up cash from the bank.

5. **Price your items.** When it comes to pricing, group items in a bin marked with one price rather than pricing each item individually. Group a number of small items together in a baggie and set a price for the whole bag. If your objective is to get rid of your stuff quickly, I recommend you price it to sell rather than set a high price with expectations of negotiating.

6. **Arrange your sale items**. Set up as much as you can on tables the night before. On the morning of your sale, simply pull out the pre-arranged tables.

   Place closely related items near each other.

   Set up larger items closer to street traffic. If the sale has worthy looking items, drivers will be motivated to stop.

   > **Bonus:** Be ready for early bird visitors; turning them away because you are not open for business could mean a lost sale.

7. **Leftover items.** Avoid bringing items that did not sell back into your home. Make arrangements for a pickup of your remaining items by the charity of your choice or load them into your car and drop off immediately after the sale is over.

The more things you own, the more they own you.

&. Unknown .&

---

33. My two-car garage is a disaster. I have no idea how to get this project started.

Garages, no matter what size, can serve as a storage area for a myriad of possessions such as bicycles, food, sports equipment, tools, garden supplies, recycling bins, overflow from the house and more. As a result of this clutter, the garage can lose its intended purpose. Which explains why the US Department of Energy reports that 25% of people with a two-car garage don't park their cars in it.

Here is your step-by-step plan to reclaim your garage:

1. **Schedule work day(s)**. First step is the sorting process, which requires you to remove everything from the garage. Check the weather forecast and schedule your work day around 1-2 consecutive days of good weather.

2. **Sort and Edit.** Work in small sections by pulling out items and sorting them on your driveway into 3 categories. (Keep — Donate — Trash/Recycling)

   - **Keep:** When you are considering items to keep — ask yourself how many of a specific item do you need? Have you used it? Will you use it and how often? If your goal is to create space, some things may need to be released in order to make that happen.

   - **Donate:** Items that fall into the 'donate' category can go to friends, family or charity. Make those deliveries promptly otherwise, these items may end up back in your garage.

   - **Recycle/Trash:** As you review your belongings, you may uncover hazardous waste items which cannot be set out with your weekly trash. These items will fall into the recycling category. To find the nearest disposal options, call your local waste carrier or visit www.earth911.com. If you're in Pennsylvania you can visit www.prc.org.

3. **Clean Sweep.** With your garage empty, give the floor a good sweep.

4. **Create Zones**. Items from the 'keep' category will go back into the garage.

   On paper or in your head, map out zones or sections in your garage so everything has a logical home based on frequency of use, grouping a category of items together and your physical space.

   Some common zones may be gardening, sports equipment, a work bench, beach/pool items, recycling area and bicycles.

5. **Store.** If your mission is to create as much floor space as possible, use the walls and overhead space for storage.

   There are DIY wall systems available at home improvement stores or you can call a closet or garage specialist.

   Garage walls are an ideal space to hang bicycles, snow shovels, outdoor folding chairs and garden equipment.

   For less frequently used items such as camp equipment or seasonal decorations, create overhead storage areas using your garage ceiling as the anchor for shelving. (ATO Pinterest board)

34. Help! Our bicycles keep falling down and hitting my car. How can we store them so they are easy to access and keep my car from getting another dent?

Even two car garages can seem spacious until the family bikes begin to encroach the space next to your car. These ideas will help create a safety net of space:

- Purchase a free-standing bike rack similar to one you'd see in a public park. It may use up a large footprint in your garage but it will keep the bicycles in place and easily accessible.

- Many homeowners prefer to have the floor space to park their car so another option is to go vertical with your storage. There are a wide variety of industrial hooks and racks available which can be installed into any wall or ceiling space in your garage.

- Lastly, utilize a combination of both ideas mentioned above. Use the bike rack during the warmer months. During the winter season when cycling is less likely an activity of choice and car protection is more of a priority, hang your bicycles and turn your unused floor bike rack on end.

> **Bonus:** Using the chin straps, hang bike helmets on the handle bar.

35. We have 4 boys involved in various sports. Any suggestions on ball storage?

Keeping balls organized may seem like an impossible task but it is a necessity so you don't get a ball stuck under your car.

Use clear or open containers which allow you to see the ball you want.

- Place a tall wire basket, such as the Gladiator Caddy, on the floor.

- Pinterest has several DIY ideas for ball storage. You can see some examples on my ATO Pinterest board.

36. My husband has woodworking tools all over his work bench. I bought him a tool box for storage but he doesn't use it. What would you recommend?

Men and their tools, *sigh*! Perhaps your husband prefers to see everything rather than hide it in a box.

Use a peg board which can be installed on the wall above his workbench. Thread U or S hooks into the pegboard holes to hold screwdrivers, pliers, hammers, etc.

Bonus: In order to help other family members, replace the tools back to the correct location after use, label the pegboard with the tool name or use a black marker to draw the outline shape of the tool on the peg board. (ATO Pinterest board)

37. Do you have any storage suggestions for some of the miscellaneous bags of grass, fertilizer, and bird seed we store in our garage?

Once opened, take these items out of their original packaging and store in metal cans or plastic 5-gallon buckets with lids. Both options can be found at hardware or home improvement stores.

Label each can for identification and store a cup inside for easy dispensing.

38. Our garage is shared space with our children. How do you suggest protecting them from the many hazardous chemicals we store in the garage?

A garage can act as a play area for children and their friends so it's up to parents to make it a safe space for them.

A lockable cabinet will keep hazardous chemicals or pesticides out of reach from children. Another option is to place these items on a shelf that is too high for your children to reach.

39. We are planning to expand our garage to include a mudroom. What should we consider when we plan out this space?

As families grow and become more active, their interest in mudroom spaces increase. A mud room is typically placed near a common entryway to the home. It is a place to remove and store muddy or wet outer wear.

Some questions you'll want to consider when planning your mudroom may include:

- How many people will be using the space?

- What you plan to store in this space will determine the storage options you choose (hooks, baskets, cubbies, etc.).

- Do you want to include a wash basin to wash off muddy clothes/shoes?

- Do you prefer storage with open shelving or closed locker style or a combination of both?

- Do you need seating to make it easier to put on and take off shoes/boots?

The important thing is to measure out enough storage that will accommodate the needs and supplies of your family year-round.

40. I travel by car for business and the two hooks in the rear seat are not enough space to hang a week's worth of dress shirts and slacks. Do you have any other storage suggestions?

A business meeting or event is off to a bad start when you walk in with wrinkled clothes.

I recommend a clothes hanger bar specifically designed for the car made by Rubbermaid®. The adjustable bar attaches to the rear seat ceiling hooks and provides as much as 5 feet of hanging space. The bar hangs low enough to provide a clear view out of the back-seat window.

If you want to prevent a single suit jacket from getting wrinkled, the Car Butler (Amazon.com) is a wooden hanger which attaches to your head rest.

41. I am a traveling sales rep and spend quite a bit of time on the road. Customer files, purchase orders, a stapler and day planner are just a few things that are rolling around in my backseat and car floor. Do you have any ideas to keep these things under control?

Having spent a number of years in outside sales, I can empathize with the chaos that can come from a mobile office. The right gear is available to help you organize your office supplies when you are limited to the space in your vehicle.

- There are mobile bags and work stations that neatly fit in the front seat of your vehicle. They can store supplies and allow you to work with the efficiency of a corner office. See examples on ATO Pinterest board.

- Incorporate a daily or weekly routine to remove trash from your mobile office and organize your client files.

- Each evening, stage your mobile office for the next day with client files and restocking of any forms or marketing material.

42. I would like to assemble an emergency kit for my daughter's car. What should I include?

Putting this kit together is similar to insurance — you hope you never need it but just in case, you are prepared.

When organizing an emergency car kit, think of being stranded in any season and any geographic area. Include the following: sun protection, traditional paper road map, compass, flash light, extra batteries, first aid supplies, fire starter and matches, a blanket, hydration (water bottles or travel water filter), repair kit/tools, nutrition (power bars, nuts, avoid chocolate items because they will melt) and an extra change of clothes, and sneakers.

*All the art of living lies in a fine mingling
of letting go and holding on.*

& Havelock Ellis &

43. We have 3 family cars and I can't remember which car had an oil change when or what car needs tires. What would you suggest to keep it all straight?

Create a vehicle maintenance log for each car to list any work performed on the car. You can store each log in the respective glove compartment. You can find a vehicle maintenance log on my website, organizationlane.com. Download it for free under the Resources tab.

The next step is follow-through. It will be the responsibility of the person taking the car in for the maintenance work to record, in the log, the work that is performed.

> **Bonus:** Be proactive when it comes to scheduling any work on your car. Plug it into your calendar and make it a recurring event. For example, when you visit the shop for an oil change, look ahead 3 months on your calendar and write or type in 'oil change'. Or look ahead one year and add 'schedule car inspection' to your calendar.

44. What organizing tools will keep my children's car stash of play things within their reach and in order?

You need to keep your eyes on the road and hands on the wheel, so reaching in the back seat to retrieve a stuffed animal or juice box is dangerous.

Search online for "back seat car caddy" and you will find various options for any age. These caddies attach to the driver or front passenger seat headrest. Some include a fold down tray and they all have numerous storage pockets. Several examples are shown on the ATO Pinterest board.

If you have two children in the back seat, you may prefer a basket positioned between them to store their favorite travel items.

45. I have four kids, all of them active and we practically live in our van. Do you have any suggestions on how I can keep the clutter in our car under control?

Today, there are many families who spend most of their time together traveling by car from one activity to another, oftentimes doing homework, eating on the run or zipping from field to field for a game or practice.

These tips can manage your car clutter:

- Keep a travel size trash can or small trash bag in your car. Empty your car of trash weekly or every time you visit the gas station for a fill up.

- Every 3 months, edit your glove compartment of any unnecessary documents and keep only your current information.

- Keep an "errand box" in your trunk. When you have deliveries, packages to mail, items to return to the store, etc. they will be one step closer to completion if it is in your car's errand box.

- To help keep things from piling up in your car, establish a *one-in-one-out* rule. If you have room for 8 DVD's in your car, bring one in and trade it for another one. The same rule applies for toys, books, sunglasses, etc.

- Use a medium size (12"x12") basket or bin to keep toys and activities together and accessible. Position the basket on the seat next to or between your children.

- For storage of more substantial items, use a laundry basket or large bin to keep items from sliding around the back seat or trunk of your car. Items such as water bottles, snacks, tissues, towels for muddy shoes, umbrella and portable chair (for cheering on the sidelines).

- Control the clutter in your console and dashboard by using a visor organizer which can be found at most auto supply stores.

KIDS AND THEIR STUFF

I have many clients who tell me how organized they were before they had children. My husband and I are empty nesters now and I will say, the time of chaos and disorder that occurs with child rearing moves at lightning speed.

Embrace it. Enjoy it. Elate in it.

In the meantime, these answers can provide some insight to a saner parenthood experience.

I'll love you forever
I'll like you for always
As long as I'm living
My baby you'll be.

❧ "Love you Forever" by Robert Munsch ❧

Time & Tasks

46. What can my husband and I do to help our children be more organized with their school work?

It is up to us, as parents, to instill positive life skills in our children as these will become vital practices once they venture into the world without us. These strategies can guide your children towards a more organized school year.

- **Use checklists.** Establish routines with the use of checklists. Create customized lists for homework, chores, nightly tasks and more. Choose your preferred medium for the checklist: whiteboard, paper, electronic or blackboard.

- **Organize notebooks.** Use a notebook and corresponding folder (for loose papers) for each subject.

  If your child responds to color cues, designate a specific color for each subject. The notebook and folder for that subject should match in color.

  > **Bonus:** To ensure your child's homework is getting completed, create two folders. One folder is homework 'to do' and the other folder is homework 'done'. Completed homework should move from the 'to do' folder to the 'done' folder each night.

- **Establish a study zone.** Create a space with necessary supplies and tools (task lighting, paper, pencils, crayons, etc.). When choosing your location, consider how much your child may need your assistance. If your child is young, has behavioral or focus issues, choose a homework location near you while you are at work in the kitchen or your desk.

- **Use a timer.** When it comes to homework, some children may be more productive working in 15 – 30-minute blocks of time and then taking a 5-minute rest. The older the child, the longer the time block.

- **Keep a Family Calendar.** Use one calendar (paper or electronic) for the family's activities. Keep a copy posted in a prominent place and encourage your children to refer to it often. Fill the calendar with activities, games, school breaks, music lessons, etc. to help establish accountability skills for the future.

- **Healthful Habits.** Provide foods high in protein and cut down on sugar. The right food choices will sustain your child's cognitive work and physical activity.

   Additionally, a restful night of sleep is an important health measure that will aid in development and focus.

> **Bonus:** Ease children into a peaceful slumber by disconnecting from all screens an hour before bedtime.

47. My children and I are always scrambling to make it to the bus stop on time. Any ideas on how to increase our success rate?

There never seems to be enough time in the morning so do as much as you can the night before.

- Choose everyone's outfit and accessories the night before and set them aside on a chair or in the closet. That includes yours too.

- Stage the following items and have them waiting at the door: shoes, coat and a fully packed back pack. Don't forget to include any school forms that need to be returned.

- Pack non-perishables in your child's lunch bag. Some perishable items can be prepared as well and stored in the refrigerator. Keep in mind that this may not work well with all foods; nobody likes a soggy sandwich.

- Review and discuss the after-school schedule/plans with your children the night before and again at breakfast. This connects a child to their daily routine and develops a sense of accountability and responsibility for their schedule.

- Prepare the coffee maker or tea kettle so you only have to turn it on in the morning.

- Place all of your ingredients into your crockpot insert for dinner and store in the refrigerator. In the morning, place the insert into your crockpot and turn it on.

48. When my children are given the task of cleaning their room, it can drag on for hours or not get done at all because they get distracted. What can I do?

Keeping a child's attention is tough these days. If they are charged with the task of doing something they do not want to do it's even harder to keep them focused. Depending on the age of your children, your presence and participation may be necessary until they are old enough to accomplish certain tasks on their own.

- Use a standard cooking timer or one of my favorite products called the Time Timer® which you can find at TimeTimer.com. Designate a reasonable number of minutes for your children to get their cleaning done before the timer ends. If they finish on time, reward them as it suits you.

- Another idea is to motivate them with high-energy music. The goal is to finish the task(s)before the song ends.

49. What advice do you have for teaching my preschooler and 2nd grader to help with household chores?

Children learn important life skills through chores. Establish routines early with small, simple tasks and organizing systems to encourage participation. For example:

- Establish a consistent routine to clean up of toys and rooms before dinner or at the end of each day.

- Use labeled baskets/bins or toy boxes to make it easier for little ones to put toys in the right place. (ATO Pinterest board)

- Use a timer to help children stay focused; explaining to your children the goal is to finish the task before the timer runs out.

- Want your child to set the table? Place dishes and cups in an area where they can reach.

- Use a checklist for accountability. Write up their chores for each day with a check box beside it. When they've completed their chore(s) they can give it a check mark of completion. You can download a free Kid's Task List on my website organizationlane.com under the Resources tab.

50. My middle school children have the same routine each school morning. Once the alarm goes off, they keep hitting the snooze button until they are late and miss the bus. I can't keep driving them to school. Any ideas?

There are many questions I have when I hear this...

- Is your child getting enough quality sleep?

- What time are they going to bed?

- What does their bedtime routine look like?

- What time are screens turned off?

Lack of sleep and a restless night are valid reasons to hit the snooze button. Assuming your children are falling asleep at a reasonable hour and getting enough sleep, **try moving their alarm clock as far away from their bed as possible**. Once it goes off, they have to get up to turn it off. Once they are up, they are more likely to stay up and get moving.

If the quality of sleep is an issue, may I recommend reading the article "Six ways to help your child get to sleep"[6] by Marissa Stapley Ponikowski in *Today's Parent*. It offers solid suggestions on how to set up a restful night of sleep for our children.

51. My high schooler is missing homework assignments because he's not writing anything down. How can I break him of this habit?

Ask your son why he's not writing down his assignments. In my experience, kids (and adults) tend to keep mental lists which is not effective in getting all tasks completed.

If your son is resisting a traditional paper planner perhaps he may prefer to use an electronic version. There are various free and paid apps available which will record, remind and track homework, for example, iStudiezPro, myhomeworkapp or Fantastical.

It's important he try the app of his choosing for at least 3 weeks — there is a learning curve to using these electronic planning tools and he shouldn't give up too soon. If he still can't seem to connect electronically then he might be more open to revisiting a paper planner.

Utilizing a daily planner teaches a necessary lifelong skill of managing time and tasks.

52. I am staying up till midnight doing homework. My mom says my phone is the problem. I don't see how a simple text to a friend which takes less than 30 seconds is cause for concern.

Sorry bud, mom's right.

In today's culture, many of us assume we need to manage both our phone and our work simultaneously, however, they strongly compete for our attention. I realize that most students have a hard time disconnecting from their phones but I can assure you, it *IS* the reason your work is not getting done.

According to a study done at the University of California Irvine,[7] distractions, as simple as a text, can delay the progress of productive work by as much as 23 minutes. While the interruption itself is only a few seconds it can take our brain much longer (up to 23 minutes) to circle back and get into the same work flow where we were prior to the interruption.

Now consider how many texts you may receive in the span of your homework time? Multiply that number by 23 minutes and that explains why you're staying up till midnight doing homework.

Here's a compromise, use a timing device (my favorite is the Time Timer®, www.timetimer.com) and set it for 30 minutes. You may want to start at 20 minutes and then work your way up to 30 minutes (or more). While the timer is running — all distracting devices (phone, computer, television) should be turned off and you get busy with your homework. When the timer is done, reward yourself with a 5-minute break.

During this break, you can check your phone, get a snack or stretch your legs. After the break is over, set the timer again, turning off all devices and work for another 30 minutes. Continue these work cycles until your homework is complete. In my experience with students (and adults) these short blocks of work time, absent of distractions, will be more productive than trying to work for hours while entertaining the countless interruptions that come from your phone. Give it a try!

Space

53. Our oldest child is off to college this year. Do you have any suggestions for setting up the dorm room?

Small spaces can be difficult to organize but not impossible. Here are a few suggestions that will help keep the clutter under control and make the most of tight quarters.

- Get more space out of the closet by using slim line hangers and/or Wonder Hangers which allow you to hang up to 5 items while using up the space of only one hanger (Amazon).

- Most college dorms offer lofted beds, but if yours does not, bed risers are an easy way to get some extra storage space underneath.

- A plastic tote caddy is ideal for carrying toiletries to the shower and keeping them contained in one place. Purchase another caddy to hold cleaning supplies.

- Under bed storage boxes can hold items that don't fit anywhere else in the room. Clear boxes make it easy to see what is stored away.

- Not all dorm rooms have a bedside table, consider a mattress or bedside caddy, which slides in-between your bed frame and mattress and hangs over the side providing various pockets of storage for a book, pencil, phone, etc. (ATO Pinterest board)

- When it comes to laundry, a hamper with wheels will ease transportation to and from the laundry room.

- Detergent pods are more convenient and take up less space than the traditional liquid or powder variety.

- Over-the-door shoe pocket organizers are great for more than just shoes. The pockets are large enough to store toiletries, socks, hats, gloves, snacks, leggings, tank tops, tools and more.

- Use 3M products: Command hooks to hang up essentials such as belts, scarves, a bath robe or pajamas; poster tabs or removable mounting putty for posters and pictures.

- Pack only the clothes needed for the season. Over Thanksgiving break, bring home summer/fall clothes and return with sweaters, coats and gloves to get through December.

54. We finally cleaned out my son's room! What can he do to prevent it from becoming cluttered again?

Every space has its limits and he needs to live within his space. Once your son's room has the right amount of stuff he needs and can store in his space then he can follow the *one-in-one-out* rule. This rule can apply to anything, clothes, shoes, books, games, toys, etc. If you buy or receive anything, something from that same category needs to be released (donated). This rule will keep everything in your son's room at its current clutter-free standing.

Collect moments not things.

❧ Unknown ❧

Toys & More

55. The generosity of my family has led to an overload of gift giving in our home and an overload of toys, books and clothes. Help!

You are not alone when it comes to the overwhelm of gifts from family members. Gift giving is an expression of love and care for another. However, if your beliefs lead you to teach your children how they can live a happy life with less stuff or you are simply running out of room in your house, then you may want to have an honest and tactful conversation with your family.

Explain how you'd like their help to implement these values with your children. Encourage them to give the gift of experiences rather than tangible items. Offer them some suggestions such as: a membership to a museum or science center, tickets to a movie, amusement park or theatrical show. A gift certificate to a favorite restaurant, bowling, ice skating or some other fun play space. Give a gift certificate to cover the cost of music or dance instruction. Family members can create their own gift certificate for a special weekend or overnight visit with them.

The vital message you want to convey to your family is that you want to see your children collect memories rather than things.

On the flip side, if your children actually do need something, be proactive and send your family a gift idea tip sheet. This will help limit the gifts to necessary and useful items. (For more on gift-giving ideas check out #126 in the Holiday chapter).

56. Toys are taking over our mid-size home. What can I do to control it?

Toys can be a blessing and a burden. Eric Clark, the author of *The Real Toy Story*, reveals a startling fact: fewer than 4% of the world's children are American, however, American children consume more than 40% of the world's toys.[8] That is an astounding figure when you think about the many children who are perfectly happy playing with the box or paper the toy was wrapped in.

Here's how to control the toy chaos in your home:

- **Establish one or two zones as designated play spaces.** Limit toys you currently own to certain spaces in the home. Toy clean up and maintenance is increased when children have free rein to roam, play and store toys in any space of your home.

- **Too many toys can be problematic.** Children can be overstimulated by the presence of too many options or develop a short attention span because they move from one toy to the next. Too many toys can also create a perception of entitlement and children can fail to grasp how much is enough.

- **Send some toys away on a "vacation."** Reduce the toys you have on hand by a percentage based on how much you own and your available play space. Send those elected toys on what I like to call "a vacation." A toy vacation is when you store toys in a bin and hide the bin elsewhere in the house. You are cutting back the number of toys for your children but still giving them enough options. In 3-6 months, make a switch of the toys on "vacation" with toys in current circulation. The vacation toys will be missed and your children will find these toys to be as engaging as when they first received them.

- **Teaching moment.** Your toy abundance can be an opportune time to teach your children the joys of charitable giving. There are a number of organizations that accept gently used toys and will give them to children who are less fortunate. A few weeks prior to your child's next birthday, Hanukkah or Christmas, work with your child to select unwanted or unused toys. Explain to your child that releasing some toys will make room for new ones he/she may receive. Share details about the charitable recipient and make a trip together to the donation drop off.

57. What is the best way to store toys?

Toy storage may evolve as a child grows and as the supply of toys grow. Toy bins and bookshelves are great storage options.

Toy Bin

- Great for large toys and they make clean up easy. However, they are not ideal for toys with small parts which tend to get lost in the bottom of a toy bin.

Bookcase

- Group similar items into baskets/bins that fit on the shelf of the bookcase. Some groupings may include: cars, dinosaurs, Barbie® accessories, LEGO elements, etc.

- Labels for baskets/bins make cleanup time easier for your kids, visiting grandparents and babysitters. This storage option also introduces your children to early organizing concepts.

> **Bonus:** If you're children are too young to read labels, attach pictures of the toy as an identifying marker of what is stored in a basket/bin. Check out the ATO Pinterest board.

- Bookcases are a piece of furniture your family will continue to find useful long after the LEGO stage of life. They can be used to store puzzles, board games, school supplies and — books!

58. We have a boy and a girl and plan to have another child in the next year. What should I do with all of the baby clothes?

Baby clothes are an investment and certainly worth hanging onto if you plan to have other children. Here's how to approach this project:

- **Sort.** Sort all clothes by size and lay them out into piles by age group and gender (newborn, 3-6 months, 6-12 months, etc.).

- **Edit.** Look through each of the piles and keep what you need. Remove anything you do not want and set aside for donation. Goodwill accepts clothes that are ripped or stained, so bag it up and let nothing go to waste.

- **Fold.** Tightly fold the clothes keeping them separated by age group and gender.

- **Pack and store.** You can place the folded items into clear plastic bins labeled accordingly. If you're tight on storage space, use a Space Bag to consolidate the clothes you've sorted and edited.

59. We've been empty nesters for a few years now. How long do we need to keep our kids' stuff?

Your home is not a storage facility for your kids' stuff. Here's how to deal with what they've left behind:

- **Last Call.** Give your kids one last chance to stake claim to any of their papers, photos, books, and mementos. Set a deadline or this conversation could go on for years. When the deadline date arrives and you have not received a response or they give you permission to make decisions on what is worth keeping, go for it!

- **Sort and Edit.** Sort through their belongings and use your judgement in keeping what is of value. Limit yourself to keep only enough items that will fit into a small box or bin.

- **What to do with it all.** Paper items you no longer wish to keep can be recycled. Books, clothes, shoes, trophies can be donated to a charity of your choice.

- **Let it Go!** The small box of items that you've decided to keep can be shipped to your son or daughter or they can bring it back home with them after their next visit with you.

Paper

60. What suggestions do you have for dealing with all of my children's artwork?

Preschool and elementary years bring a deluge of artwork into the home. If you're like me, you feel the need to save them. You'll carefully store them in a special portfolio. You think it will be so much fun to look at the art pieces together when your child turns 18. Stop right there! Here's how my story ended.

When my daughter was 15, I took a peek in that portfolio and was shocked to see the deterioration of her artwork. The noodles were breaking off, paper was turning yellow and the paint was fading. In a few years, there would be nothing recognizable to show my daughter. This was the moment I realized I needed a change in strategy. Based on my personal experience, here's what I tell my clients now:

- **Share your child's artwork.** You do not have to be the only beneficiary of your child's masterpieces. Mail artwork to grandparents, Godparents, babysitters and other relatives; it is a thoughtful gesture that will be appreciated.

- **Frame special pieces** and hang them in your home or give them as gifts to grandparents.

- **Use an artist portfolio** (available at craft stores) to temporarily store special pieces until you decide how you plan to use them. They are ideal for those large poster size pieces.

- **Digitally preserve the artwork.** Take photos of your child's artwork and when you are ready you can toss out the physical artwork. I know what you're thinking — you don't have to toss out the artwork right away. Store them for as long as you like and check on them in a few years. You will eventually come to terms with the realistic notion as I did, that the physical pieces of art will not last and preserving them digitally is the best solution.

- **Permanent storage.** If you decide you can't let go of their artwork, then store it permanently in envelopes or boxes that are acid and lignin free. Various options are available online.

- **Enjoy and explore the possibilities with digital photos.** Once you've captured the artwork digitally, you can create a variety of fun projects, such as coffee mugs, coasters, calendars, and more.

Here's how my story ended...after I photographed all of my children's work, I made each of them a hard cover book filled with photos of their artwork and presented it to them as a Christmas gift. The book captured and preserved their artwork in a form they can share with their children. Photo websites such as Forever.com and Shutterfly allow you to create a variety of gifts and functional items that all begin with a piece of art.

61. School is starting again in two weeks. Can you offer some advice to help me manage my family in a more organized way?

There are three areas that parents need to manage in preparation for the surge of paper and scheduling that lies ahead with the start of a new school year. Paper storage, routines and calendar use.

Paper Storage

Brace yourself! During the first few weeks of school your child will come home with dozens of forms and reminders in their backpacks. It all needs to go somewhere and the dining room table is not the best solution. Instead, create a file system. Here's how:

- Begin with a hanging file labeled with your child's name.

- Insert file folders labeled with your child's activities. For example: music lessons, scouts, band, soccer and basketball. Create a folder for school papers and another for physicals. These file folders will be stored within your child's main hanging file. Any paper, related to that activity now has a home.

Bonus: Make extra copies of your child's immunization and physical forms to have on hand to submit to any group, sport or club that makes the request.

Paper Routine

Once your filing system is in place, develop a daily routine to manage the paper that flows through your house. Executing this routine everyday will prevent major piles from ever forming. Your routine will require you to sort through backpacks every day. File away documents into their designated folders, toss out the unnecessary papers and take action on anything else.

This will be your job to handle when your children are young but eventually they should be taking ownership of this task. The file system is designed to be user friendly and you are establishing a useful life skill your child will need.

> **Bonus:** Edit school files over winter break and again at the end of the school year.

Calendar Use

- Download/sync the school calendar to your smart phone or mark your paper calendar with any early release dates, holidays, sports schedules etc.

- Day Planner — Most schools issue a day planner for your child. This is a great tool to teach your child homework/project planning and time management. Help your child make the most of this planner by including after school activities.

62. My children recently completed 6th and 8th grade. I've always had trouble deciding what to do with all of their school papers and awards at the end of the year.

No matter what grade has been completed, create a memory box for each child.

Keep only school papers that are worthy of being a part of the memory box. Which goes back to your original question...how to decide what's worth keeping. Let's face it, in 20 years when you dig through this memory box, your child is unlikely to care about his 4th grade math homework. However, he might enjoy seeing his handwriting and reading his book report from 4th grade. In other words, set limits on how much to keep by choosing the best pieces that reflect who your child is at this stage of his life.

Store documents for each school year in an acid and lignin free envelope or folder (available from Amazon) and label them accordingly. Include the year, favorite teacher, best friends, etc. A memory box is a great place to store other special keepsakes such as a baptism outfit, first shoes and more. Be mindful of how much you keep and limit your collection to one container per child.

Choose a container that best suits the climate or conditions where it will be stored. I always lean towards clear plastic bins with tight locking lids.

Bonus: Ready to reduce the volume of keepsakes? If you digitally capture your child's mementos you can release the physical objects. This is great for bulky items such as trophies, which can take up a good deal of space.

63. I would like to set up a centralized area to store all of my kids/family scheduling information. Can you offer some guidance as to how to do this?

Taking the time to set up what's typically referred to as Family Command Center will help save you time in the long run. As the term implies, this is your family's base of operations; where all information will pass through. Here's how to set up your own Command Center:

- Find an ideal location. Since all family members will be delivering information to the command center, it will be more likely to work if it is set up in a central part of your home. For many families, the kitchen or family room is a convenient place.

- The space for the command center can be a small desk, the inside of a cabinet, or the corner surface area of a kitchen counter. See question #6.

- Set up a filing system to hold your family's day-to-day documents. The files located in the command center should be current and active items only. Older, inactive items can be archived and stored elsewhere in the home. See question #61, paper storage.

- Utilize one family calendar. Multiple calendars in a home increase the possibility of double booking or missing appointments. When you receive a schedule for school, an activity, sports team, etc., upload for electronic calendars or fill in important dates on the paper calendar immediately.

- Outfit your command center with the necessary tools to efficiently manage and complete your tasks. For example, a file holder, phone, calendar, shopping list, chore charts, envelopes, stamps, check book, pens, markers, address book, stapler, white board, etc.

TIME MANAGEMENT / PRODUCTIVITY

The tagline for my business is *Getting you on the Road to Productivity,* because no matter who you are — a mom, entrepreneur, student or business professional — when you can manage the physical and mental parts of your life, you will be more productive.

It's not enough to be busy, so are the ants.
The question is "What are we busy about?"

∾ Henry David Thoreau ∾

Time & Tasks

64. I manage my to-do items in one of two ways: 1) store them in my head; or 2) write them down on various slips of paper which are scattered everywhere. Neither method works well. What can I do?

Research tells us that our brains are not meant to be a holding tank for our errands, projects, or to-do items. Mentally storing these tasks and thoughts does two things:

1. We become distracted in the present moment because of our preoccupation with trying to remember everything.

2. Decreases the likelihood that every task rolling around in your head will get accomplished. You're bound to miss something.

David Allen, the author of *Getting Things Done,*[9] suggests that we move tasks out of our head and record them externally so they will be more likely to get done. My short answer — do a brain dump.

Use all or a combination of the following tools to capture your thoughts:

- **Calendar**. Whether you use a paper or electronic calendar, utilize it for more than just traditional appointments. Include reminders that regularly repeat such as: your pet's monthly heart worm pill, annual mammogram, yearly car inspection, yearly shut down of an outdoor water valve, or signing up for next year's college housing. Stop storing it in your head and schedule it in your calendar. If you are using an electronic calendar, hit the repeat notification and you'll never have to think about it again.

- **Categorized Master List.** You can use a notepad for this list or an electronic application if you prefer. Divide your master list into categories of interest, work and service. Write down your tasks below each category. This division of tasks will make it easier to see what needs to get done. Over the course of a week or two, you will cross off tasks as they are completed and add new tasks under the specified category. When the list starts to look untidy, transfer the tasks to a new page on the notepad and begin again.

- **Daily List.** This list is your game plan for what you will do today. To keep the lists unified, I would use a page that follows the

categorized master list in the same notepad. Check your calendar and reflect on the time you need for scheduled appointments, meetings or classes. Any free blocks of time in the day will allow you to work on tasks you choose from your categorized master list. Create your daily list by writing down 1-4 tasks to accomplish for today. When those tasks are complete, you will cross them off your daily list and the categorized master list as well. Limit your daily tasks to a conservative number. You can always add items to the list later if you finish with time to spare.

- **Shopping List.** Whether you need bread, a present for a birthday party, or a white shirt for your son's concert, write it down on a shopping list. Everyone in the family can help create this list so keep it in a commonly accessed area of your house. If your kids use the last of the cereal, then they are responsible for writing it on the shopping list.

> **Bonus:** Divide your shopping list into categories by the store to simplify the logistics of your shopping. For example, Target, Grocery store, Costco, vegetable market, etc.

- **Someday List.** These are items that we tend to store in our head which do not fit on any of the aforementioned lists and yet we do not want to forget about them. For example, your daughter expresses an interest in a book, however, her birthday is not for several months. Write it down on the someday list. Or a friend raved about a travel agent who took care of their trip to Italy. You and your husband plan to go to Italy but not for a few years. Write the name and contact information of the travel agent on your someday list.

Tech Options — if you prefer to use an electronic list-making tool there are many available with new ones coming out every month. Some tried and true apps include Wunderlist, Evernote, Todoist and Any.do.

Remember, use these tools to empty your head of thoughts, capture them so they are not forgotten, and increase the likelihood they get done.

65. Distractions are getting in the way of completing my work. How do I manage this problem?

Being productive at work goes beyond achieving a healthy bottom line for your employer. When we are productive at work, we finish on time and can make it to our kid's soccer game. We are recognized for our achievements which can result in position and financial advancements. Our stress and anxiety are decreased, and that is a healthier way to live.

Distractions such as our phone, the internet and television impede our progress with work because of the constant attention we tend to give to these devices. I tell my clients, while doing focused work, turn them off. Period.

While we cannot work a full day without our devices, the compromise is to work in time blocks. Set a timer for 30-45 minutes and work without any distractions, then take a 5-minute break. Check your device during your break for anything you've missed. Reset your timer and start working again.

Working in short, uninterrupted blocks of time is more productive and provides you with the focus required to move the needle forward on your project. See #52 for more information.

66. Help! I'm busy doing stuff but my to-do list is still full at the end of the day. What am I doing wrong?

I'll admit, every once in a while, I'm guilty of this myself. We are completing tasks; however, they are not tasks on our list. This is procrastination at work!

Sometimes we can occupy ourselves with tasks in order to avoid doing a more critical or not so pleasant task. Try this... determine when you have the most energy in your day. Harness that natural energy and work on your least favorite or most difficult tasks during that time.

Brian Tracy, author of *Eat that Frog!*,[10] suggests your "frog" is the biggest or most unpleasant task of the day. Instead of putting it off, go ahead and eat your frog first and then work on other tasks.

Lists simplify, clarify, edify.

&ᴖ Tom Peters ᴖ&

---

67. I'm feeling overwhelmed at work, I can't seem to keep up. Any suggestions?

Being overwhelmed and stressed out is not productive for your employer and it's unhealthy for your body. In order to lighten your work load, is it possible to outsource or delegate some of your responsibilities?

Delegation requires that we relinquish control and trust that others can accomplish tasks on our behalf. It will free you up to focus your attention on a task only you can manage. Effective delegation is an integral part of leadership and builds a supportive working environment.

In order to ensure an effective execution, delegate a task to someone you trust who has a proven track record. Provide your chosen candidate with comprehensive and clear instructions. The more details you share, the easier it is to understand and complete the delegated task. Be sure to include any important deadlines, contact information, and then let it go!

This example of delegation was framed with the workplace in mind, however, delegation is applicable in the home. Delegating the tasks of cleaning, cooking, laundry, landscaping or babysitting to family members or outside sources can help a stressed-out mom or dad too.

68. I lose track of time and never seem to have enough?

Integrating time management skills into our day requires that we learn new behaviors and practice them regularly until they become second nature.

These tips will help you become a better manager of time and make the most of the day:

- **Use analog clocks.** Digital clocks only show time in the present. Analog clocks display time with rotating hour and second hands. This creates time awareness by seeing time move which improves the understanding of how long it takes to do something. I recommend putting analog clocks in every room, especially the bathroom!

- **Use a planner/calendar.** for assignments and appointments. Mastering this tool is an essential skill that begins in school and continues through life.

- **Use a time Tracking Worksheet** for a week. A close watch on how and where you spend your time may enlighten you to where time is being wasted. This exercise is a good lesson in understanding how long it takes to complete tasks. Print off a copy of a Time Map Chart at organizationlane.com under the Resources tab.

- **Assign time estimates to tasks.** Once you've written your to-do list, assign a time estimate for how long it will take to complete each task. Accurate estimates will become easier with practice. Time estimating will prevent you from over-scheduling your day and increase your focus on each task.

Nothing will work unless you do.

❧ Maya Angelou ❧

---

69. We still use a paper calendar in our house. Do you have any suggestions for our family of 5 when it comes to making the calendar work for us?

Paper or electronic — it doesn't matter. A family calendar is essential to keeping tabs on everyone's whereabouts. It makes it possible to plan a family gathering. Your kids are also learning a valuable principle by your example.

Here's how to make the most of your family calendar:

- Utilize only one calendar. Some folks try to manage more than one calendar and will inevitably miss writing down an appointment in one calendar and end up double booking a time slot.

- Keep your calendar in a visible place where everyone in the family gathers. This central location will encourage the rest of the family to be involved with their schedules. Some common locations are the refrigerator or a kitchen message board.

- Make appointments visually stand out on your calendar, by using a different color highlighter for each family member. Younger children can connect to their schedule through these visual cues until they can read.

- Use the calendar to mark down all timely "to do" items that may be stored in your head. Tasks such as giving your pet his heart worm pill each month, changing the furnace filter, car inspections, etc.

- When you receive your child's school schedule, take the time to mark down any early release or school closing dates. You'll have plenty of time to arrange for child care, if necessary.

Bonus: If you use an electronic calendar, check to see if your child's school district has the capability to sync with your phone. This feature will save you time by instantly loading school events, games and concerts into your calendar.

Making Time

70. I wish I could say "no" but I'm a people pleaser. What can I do to stop my compulsive "yes" behavior?

While you want to help others, it may be at the expense of your own well-being, family and general productivity. When we say 'yes', we are saying 'no' to something else.

Consider these thoughts to create your '**no strategy**':

- **Think first.** Oftentimes, we say yes because we don't know what else to say. When you're in the moment, saying yes is just plain easier to do. When someone asks you to volunteer for something, refrain from giving them an immediate response. Instead, simply say "May I please take the night to think about it?" Or "I'll have to check my calendar for availability and get back to you."

  Then take the time to consider these questions: Are you interested in taking on this task? Do you have the time? What sacrifices will need to be made? Are you passionate about this cause? Once you've formulated your answer, reach out to the person who asked you and share your thoughtful response. Never say yes without taking the time to thoughtfully consider what you are agreeing to.

- **Practice makes perfect.** This may sound a little silly but I tell my clients to write down on paper a generalized 'no' response. Craft your own response so it reflects your personality and sincerity. Practice what you've written. Get comfortable with it. Use this prepared response when you need it.

- **Discern**. I'm not suggesting you shouldn't volunteer to help others or exercise your philanthropic goals. I am suggesting you take the time to determine what is the best way to use the time in your day. Recognize that you have the power to say 'yes' or 'no' which will determine how your day(s) are shaped.

71. What can I do to carve out some "me-time"?

You are not alone. We live in a culture where we tend to over-schedule ourselves leaving very little or no time for self-care. Treat your 'me-time' like any other traditional appointment, schedule it in your calendar. Whether it's a yoga class, read a book, coffee with a friend, pedicure, massage, you name it — write it in your calendar and you will be more likely to keep that appointment.

72. I never seem to have time to read anymore. How can I find a little sliver of time to enjoy a good book?

Don't drop out of your book club yet. With a little advance planning you can still enjoy reading a good book.

- Take public transportation to work or school which will allow you the freedom to read while someone else is driving.

- Plan ahead and bring your book while waiting in a doctor's office or walking on a treadmill.

- Change your daily routine by getting to bed a little earlier to read before falling asleep. Or set your alarm a little earlier and begin your day with some reading.

73. I recently started a part-time job and I can't find time to plan, shop or make meals for my family. Any suggestions?

The term "working mom" has always been a bit of a contradiction to me since I believe, every mom works!! When you combine it with paid work then you have a mom working double time.

These ideas have been helpful to me and other moms who have returned to the paid workforce or started a business:

- **Schedule one day** to plan out meals for your upcoming week. Review your child's after school activities for the week as this may determine if you need to plan a meal on the go. My website has a free printable weekly menu plan. Go to organizationlane.com under the Resources page.

- **Review recipes** to help create your shopping list so you don't miss an important ingredient.

- **Write up your shopping list** according to the layout of the store. This will help you use your time in the store as efficiently as possible.

- **Keep coupons**, if you use them, attached to your list.

> **Bonus:** Use the front of an envelope as your shopping list and store the coupons inside.

- **Double a recipe.** Freeze the second portion and you have a meal ready to go for later that month.

- **Use your crock pot** all year long. There are various websites you can search for crock pot recipes. One of my favorites is 365daysofcrockpot.com.

- **Salad in a snap.** Spend a little extra time chopping all of your vegetables for salads at one time. You can store chopped peppers, cucumbers and onions in an air-tight container. Toss a handful of cut vegetables with pre-washed lettuce into a bowl and you have a salad in less than a minute.

- **Easy recipes at your fingertips.** Search the internet using the terms "quick recipes" or "5 ingredients or less recipes." Collect these easy recipes to help broaden your menu options.

- **Recruit your kids for help.** Based on their age and ability, they can set the table, get a part of the meal started or prepare the salad.

- **Designate one night a week for a favorite easy meal.** Be sure to keep those ingredients stocked in your pantry. For the Lane family, it's Taco Tuesday!!

- **Keep staples on hand.** If you have a day that does not go as planned, it's nice to reach into your pantry for a few staples to prepare a quick stand-by meal. For example, pasta and sauce or grilled cheese and canned soup.

- **Rinse and repeat.** When you have created 3-4 weeks of menu plans, simply repeat it. Remember, the reason behind the meal is to bring your family together and to provide them with nourishment.

74. My fellow co-workers stop into my office to visit while I'm working. What can I do to prevent this without being rude to them?

This kind of interruption affects your focus which impacts your productivity. Try any one of these options to tactfully deal with unscheduled visitors:

- If you have a door to your office, close it. Place a note on the outside of the door or on the back of your chair (if you work in a cubicle) which reads "Focused Work in Progress, Please Do Not Disturb." This sends a clear message that you are actively working and cannot be interrupted.

- If you work in a shared, open space try wearing earbuds or noise cancelling headphones. Whether you listen to music or not, people are less likely to bother you.

- Be gracefully honest. Let your visitor know that you are working against a deadline but you do want to connect. Try to schedule a lunch or coffee date to catch up so you can give them your full attention.

75. Help, I'm addicted to checking my email constantly.

Checking and replying to emails the moment you hear the notification ping is a responsive habit that can impede your overall productivity. It not only interrupts your plan of scheduled tasks, but it sends a message that you are readily available and reply instantaneously. Email is not instant messaging and should be handled differently.

I suggest implementing these strategies to curb your immediate response to emails:

- **Establish response time.** Recognize that nearly any email reply can wait a few hours. Professional courtesy suggests a 24-hour response time. Stop dropping everything you're doing to answer an email.

- **Set up designated check times.** Throughout the day check and reply to emails at scheduled times. A good rule of thumb is mid-morning, after lunch and just before you leave the office. Be sure to build in time for the task of replying and cleaning up your inbox.

- **Turn off notifications.** When you need to do focused work, turn off any auditory or visual notifications for email in order to avoid the distraction of what's happening with your inbox.

Bonus: Ease into this new habit of not immediately responding to email, by using your vacation reply feature. Your message can read: "Thank you for your email. I am in the office, however, checking my email on a limited basis. I will get back to you within one business day."

Provide an alternate option to connect with you, if needed.

Be More Productive

76. What tips do you have for running an effective meeting?

A meeting without direction and leadership will accomplish nothing but waste the time of people attending the meeting. It's up to the leader to set the stage for success of the meeting. Whether it's for your local parent/teacher group or a meeting of board executives here are proven strategies to use:

1. **Begin with a purpose.** What objectives do you have for your meeting? Be sure your goals are clearly conveyed in your meeting invite and agenda.

2. **Invite with intention.** Do not waste someone's time by inviting them to a meeting if they don't have to be there. Choose meeting participants that are connected to or can help achieve your meeting goals. Send out an email to invite participants to your meeting include the meeting time, date, length of the meeting, overall purpose, and location.

3. **Send out your meeting agenda in advance.** This gives participants a chance to review the meeting objectives and come prepared with ideas and questions to share.

4. **Start and end on time.** Waiting on latecomers, is not only disrespectful to those participants who arrive on time, but also sets a precedent that it is acceptable to arrive late.

5. **Manage time.** While you want to encourage open communication during the meeting, it is important the discussion stays on track with the agenda objectives. If someone gets off track, acknowledge their statements or concerns and make a suggestion to address them at another time in order to stay focused on the current topic and your meeting timeline.

6. **Review action steps.** At the close of your meeting be sure to review any follow up steps you expect from participants.

7. **Send out minutes** within 24 hours of your meeting. Highlight the action steps in red or use a bold face font so they can be easily seen and followed through with a higher success rate.

77. My husband is a perfectionist. He can never finish a project in our house because he is obsessed with everything being just right. Is there anything I can do to help him?

This question reminds me of a quote by Michael J. Fox: "I am careful not to confuse excellence with perfection. Excellence I can reach for; perfection is God's business." It's up to your husband to understand the consequences of his perfectionism and to weigh those consequences against the acceptance of realistic goals.

You could begin with a conversation with these talking points:

- Perfectionism is a productivity killer. Perfectionism can lead to procrastination and that can interfere with a project deadline. I love the phrase: "Done is better than none." If a perfectionist becomes caught up in creating something perfect or delays the start of a project waiting for perfect conditions, ultimately, the project will not be completed in a timely manner. This can result in repercussions at work and in relationships. Acceptance of a completed project is better than no project at all.

- Incorporate Julie Morgenstern's Max-Mod-Min[11] technique. Define the details of the project or task that can be completed in each level of performance. What is the maximum, moderate, and minimum you could do for a project? Choose a level that will fit into your schedule and stick with it.

- Being a perfectionist can be damaging to one's self-esteem. Can you imagine the stress, depression and anxiety that come with the responsibility of being perfect? To help alleviate that stress, your husband can map out a detailed plan of approach for a project. Be sure this plan includes time-sensitive deadline markers to achieve at each step. This plan will help create a sense of clarity while maintaining a high level of focus because it is task oriented with deadlines. (See question #79; **Backwards Planning** is a helpful project planning tool to consider.)

78. I volunteered to take on a large project. I have no idea where to start so I haven't started at all and the deadline is quickly approaching. What can I do?

Think of a big project as a whole cake. Under normal circumstances, you would not eat a whole cake in one sitting. Right? Remember I said normal circumstances. You would eat one piece on one day. Then the next day, you would eat another piece and so on, until the cake was finished.

Break your project down into small, bite-size chunks.

- Create a detailed list of all tasks that are required to complete this project from beginning to end.

- Use a note pad or go digital with Asana, Trello, Allthings, or other project management application.

- Integrate one or two tasks at a time into your day as your schedule permits. Be mindful of your overall deadline. This will keep the long list of tasks from overwhelming you.

79. I have a fundraising project that will require some long-term planning. This is not my strong suit; how can I get it done in a timely manner?

Any long-term project would fall under the category of big project planning. As mentioned in the prior question, the first step in planning is to break the project down into small tasks and then follow these steps:

1. Once a list of each task is created then I recommend you use a project planning strategy common in business known as **backward planning**.

2. The next step is to review your calendar, marking the actual due date of the project and then create your own due date a week earlier from the actual due date. This self-imposed deadline allows for trouble shooting problems or unexpected delays that may arise.

3. Looking at your calendar, begin with your self-imposed due date and working backwards write in a task or two from your project list for each day and work backwards towards today. If something comes up and a task needs to be shifted to another day, you've created that safety net of time with the self-imposed deadline.

80. I'm so sluggish in the afternoon and find I'm getting less work done. Any ideas?

The human body is amazing! It responds and reacts based on how we treat it and feed it. When you feel sluggish, give yourself a self-care scan.

You are what you eat.

- Incorporate high-protein snacks in your day such as a handful of nuts, hard-boiled egg or yogurt. Foods high in protein facilitate brain function.

- Try eating smaller more frequent meals throughout the day to sustain your energy verses eating three large meals.

- Drink water rather than sugary or caffeinated beverages.

Add movement to your day.

- Get up from your desk and stretch.

- Take the stairs instead of the elevator.

- Park far away from the entrance and walk.

- Find other ways to squeeze in movement throughout your day.

The power of sleep.

- According to the Sleep Foundation[12] less than 8 hours of sleep (for adults) is considered sleep deprivation and can lead to a number of negative health consequences including ineffective long and short-term memory, weight gain, depression, diabetes, high blood pressure and more. Our bodies use sleep to renew, recharge and revive for another day of work and play. Getting to bed at a reasonable hour should be a daily priority.

To create is to live twice.

❦ Albert Camus ❧

73

81. I have over 8,000 emails in my inbox. What can I do to make my inbox more manageable?

Having a cluttered inbox is similar to a cluttered desk filled with piles of paper. You may miss or lose an important message or task because it is buried amongst a few hundred or thousands of emails. Here's how to bring your inbox to a manageable place and keep it there:

- **Unsubscribe.** Recognize that unwanted emails are a source of your digital clutter and take action to keep them out. Just like junk mail, you can unsubscribe from newsletters, blogs, advertisements and coupons. I recommend using a mass unsubscribe tool such as Unsubscriber from Other Inbox or Unroll.me. You simply register your email address and the tool will automatically create a folder for you to drag and drop any emails that you no longer wish to receive and they will take steps to unsubscribe for you. Both of these apps are free. ☺

- **Delete.** If you are dealing with a backlog of emails, dedicate 10 minutes each day to deleting the unwanted emails starting with the oldest ones first.

- **Update Notifications.** Turn off email notifications for social media sites. These emails are only adding to your digital clutter. You will get the updates you need when you check your Facebook, Twitter or Linked In pages. Having these notifications come to your inbox is redundant.

- **Rethink your Inbox.** Many people tend to use their email inbox as a visual "to do" list. In other words, if an email is still sitting in your inbox then it is something you need to do. When it's done, you delete or file the email away. This system is effective only for some folks but for those who receive more than 50 emails/day it can be difficult to see what is a priority as it may move off the first page. Remember, *out of sight is out of mind.*

- **Categorize.** Create folders to help prioritize and categorize all of your emails. The folders can be labeled by action, (follow-up, call, weekly tasks, etc.), subject (child's name, group name, sport, etc.), project (fundraiser, musical, auction, etc.), date or a combination of categories. Once you've created your folders, you can read the email, take action and then move it to the appropriate folder. This will keep your inbox clear and still allow you to keep the information on hand.

Bonus: Go to Zero. Want to get a fresh start but don't have the time to edit your entire inbox? Create a folder that is dated with the oldest to the newest email in your inbox. Drag all emails to this folder and whalah! You are now at zero and can begin integrating these new email strategies from a clear inbox. Don't worry, all those emails are in a safe place if you ever need them.

82. I am a master at multi-tasking; I've read that it's not a productive way to work, why?

Multi-tasking was an accepted and encouraged work style for years. However, research indicates it is not a productive way to work.

- The term multi-tasking suggests we are working on two tasks at the same time but actually we are not. When we multi-task we are actually task switching and doing it at high speeds so we think we are working on two tasks simultaneously. When it comes to working on two cognitive tasks, it is impossible for us to work on them both effectively.

  I'll use this example to illustrate...when you are writing an email and you receive a phone call, you are not proficiently working on both tasks. There are moments when you're listening or talking and not writing your email. Or you're writing but not listening. What we're really doing is phasing in and out of working on each task. We are dividing our attention between the two tasks and not giving either task 100% effort — that is not productive.

- People assume multi-tasking saves time because we are performing two tasks at once. However, it takes longer to complete both tasks because our brain needs more time to switch gears from one task to another.

- Multi-tasking increases your chances of mistakes. Scientists at the Institut National de la Sante et de la Recherche Medicale (INSERM)[13] in Paris discovered this when they asked participants to complete two tasks at the same time while undergoing a functional MRI. The results show the brain splits in half and causes us to forget details and make three times more mistakes.

- Multi-tasking is a brain drain. When we are in a constant state of task switching it overloads the demands on our brain, zaps our cognitive resources and decreases our sharpness. This can also make us more tired and may be the reason why we are yearning for a mid-day cup of coffee.

- Finally, it's unhealthy. Multi-tasking puts our bodies in a state of high-alert which causes a release of stress hormones. Working under these conditions long term can negatively affect your body.

Rather than multi-tasking, employ the use of **task batching**. Where the focus is on grouping tasks that require the same mindset. Schedule work in 30-minute time blocks dedicated to a certain batch of tasks. In other words, perform research in a time block, write emails, make phone calls and pay bills in their own batch. In the end, task batching enables you to produce quality work and make the best use of your time.

OFFICE / PAPER

While we live in a digital culture, we are not yet a paperless society. Mail, newspapers, catalogs, coupons, junk mail, school and business papers are a consistent source of angst for many. This never-ending flow of paper also brings to light, a number of important questions.

For every minute spent organizing, an hour is earned.

– Benjamin Franklin –

83. Is there a way to stop receiving junk mail?

According to the Center for Development of Recycling at San Jose State University, each American adult receives **41 pounds of junk mail per year!**[14]

I cannot guarantee the junk mail will stop completely but you will see a significant reduction. This information comes from the Federal Trade Commission website (www.ftc.gov)

- To stop unsolicited direct mail, register your address at www.dmachoice.org.

- To stop prescreened credit offers from filling your mailbox, register your address at www.optoutprescreen.org.

- To stop catalogs, visit www.catalogchoice.org. You can specifically select the catalogs you no longer wish to receive.

Allow 30-90 days for your requests to be processed.

> **Bonus:** Paper Karma is a free application for your smart phone that will allow you to photograph the address page of your junk mail and they will make attempts, on your behalf, to unsubscribe you from the mailing list.

84. I like to bookmark magazines when I find something of interest. However, I waste time searching for what I wanted to save in the magazine. Can you suggest a more organized system?

We all have good intentions when we purchase a magazine subscription; we plan to re-decorate, get crafty, or try the latest exercises or recipes. However, if you have piles of magazines collected throughout your house, it's nearly impossible to efficiently search and retrieve what you want when you want it.

In order to have the article or recipe of interest at your fingertips tear it out of the magazine and slide it into a clear sheet protector (available at office supply stores) and collect them into a 3-ring binder. Create reference binders for different subjects of interest (crafts, food, decorating, fitness, etc.) and use divider tabs to separate categories within the subject. For example, in a recipe binder you can include tabs for: appetizers, meatless dishes, crock pot meals, desserts, etc. Retrieval of information is then effortless and streamlined.

Once you've collected your favorite ideas from the magazine, there is no reason to keep the magazine. Toss it into the recycling bin.

> **Bonus:** If you are ready to make the move from paper to digital idea collection — Pinterest has everything you need from health to hobbies. With Pinterest, you have eliminated the need for any magazines. (Pinterest.com)

85. I need to regain some space on my shelves. I'm ready to let go of some books — what can I do with them?

Books are delightful treasures. They can be hard to release, but if you no longer have the space to keep them all, letting some of them go becomes a necessity. Remember, they gave you joy and pleasure at one time and now you can share that joy with someone else.

Check with your local library. Many public libraries hold sales from book donations collected throughout the year. Nursing homes and prisons also welcome book donations. The Antiquarian Booksellers at www.abaa.org is a good source for donating antique books.

Options for selling books for cash include: Half-Price books and cash4books.net.

> **Bonus:** If you love the book and need the book shelf space, acquire an electronic version.

> **Double Bonus:** If you're crafty and would like to repurpose your books for decorative or functional uses, visit the ATO Pinterest board for some clever ideas.

Out of clutter, find simplicity.

❧ Albert Einstein ☙

---

86. What advice do you have to help me keep my desk in order?

If your desk is killing your advancement opportunities or making it impossible to keep up with the paper flow, you are not alone. According to CareerBuilder.com, 33% of office workers say they tend to be hoarders. And, 28% of employers say they would be less likely to promote someone with a disorganized or messy workspace.[15]

Here are my thoughts on creating a productive desk:

- Keep a conservative quantity of supplies you will use or need at your desk. For example, 23 yellow highlighters in your pencil drawer seems like overkill. Instead, keep what you need and store the remaining highlighters in your company's supply room.

- Create a filing system with current/active documents only, this makes it easy to *file* away papers and to *find* them later. (See #96)

- If you need more file space, archive older files. Any documents that are not in current use can be stored in cardboard file boxes or another file cabinet elsewhere in the office. (Check your company's retention policy)

- Arrange tools on your desk based on their frequency of use. Items you use most often should be closer to you and those items you use less frequently can be placed further away. Placement of frequently used items can impact your physical comfort, so be mindful if you are left or right handed when deciding where to place your phone, adding machine, computer mouse and screen, etc.

- Don't let personal mementos take over your desk space. While we enjoy keeping our loved ones close, your desktop can quickly become cluttered with art projects and framed photos if you do not exercise some discretion.

Bonus: There are some alternative options to repurpose mementos while still having them provide functionality to your work space. Take digital pictures of artwork or family members and create a customized calendar, mouse pad, coffee mug or pencil cup.

87. What is the best system for incoming mail? I inevitably end up with a large pile of mail on my dining room table at the end of each week.

Mail is a major contributor to the paper clutter in a home or office. Allowing mail to accumulate, even for a couple of days is what can get the snowball to form. Your first line of defense is to sort through your mail each day.

- Sort your mail daily and place it into one of 3 categories. (File Away — Take Action — Toss)

  o **File Away.** Documents you need for future reference will be filed away, therefore, you'll need to create a file system (see #96). Ideally, it is best to file your papers as they come in. If you do not have the time, then have a bin or basket to hold papers temporarily that need to be filed away. Be mindful of your filing duties or this bin will grow into two bins.

  o **Take Action**. Some possible action steps are a phone call, write a check or sign and return a document. These follow up items can be stored in a basket or bin but it's important that they are not forgotten, so add these tasks to your daily to do list.

  o **Toss.** The last category includes any item that can be considered trash. In this case, recycle your paper or shred if the paper contains any personal information. Experts vary in the advice on what's considered "personal." A good rule of thumb is documents that have your name, address or any full or partial numbers related to your banking, finance and social security.

- Create a permanent home for each of these piles or else they will be back on the dining room table.

Using a new paper management discipline may take several weeks to become a habit. Be patient and do your best to stick with it. The piles of mail should only appear when you've returned from a vacation.

If nothing changed, there'd be no butterflies.

❧ Unknown ❧

---

88. I just started a home-based business and need a system to organize my tax paperwork, what would you suggest?

Establishing a file system of tax related documents for your home-based business is good practice as it will save you time come April.

- Create a recording sheet for each month of the year which includes the following categories: income, expenses and business/tax related. Mark down any transactions each month related to the appropriate category.

- Keep a corresponding envelope or folder with pockets for each month which will hold any supportive documents related to the transaction you recorded. An accordion binder is another option for compiling these documents.

At the end of the year you will have a concisely written record for each month referencing income, expenses and taxes along with the accompanying documents ready for your accountant. He/she will thank you for it.

> **Bonus:** Want to go digital? Here are some software options to manage your finances: Quicken, Quick Books and Mint.com

89. How do you suggest filing important documents such as birth certificates, passports, etc.?

These hard to replace documents require extra protection and sometimes quick retrieval. I recommend you place birth certificates, social security cards, marriage license, passports, insurance policies in clear protective sheets and store in a 3-ring binder. Keep the binder in a **fire-proof safe**.

> **Bonus:** Another item I recommend to include in your binder is a copy, front and back, of all credit cards you possess. If your wallet is ever stolen, canceling all of your cards will be simple when you have the contact information secured in one place.

90. Where should I store all of my computer passwords?

On my website, organizationlane.com, there is a free checklist under the Resources tab with a password log. Keep this log in a safe and protected place near your computer.

A small address book can alphabetically store your passwords. Again, keep that book in a safe place.

Lastly, there are free apps which can securely store and manage all of your passwords and will also give you access to them remotely. Dash Lane (no relation), Robo Form and Sticky Pass are just a few.

91. We have so many photos stored in various places of my home. I'm ready to finally get them organized but I'm not sure what's the best way to start.

The average family accumulates 3,000 printed photos each year.[16] Organizing printed photos is a daunting task that should be approached in small steps.

Here's your step by step guide to get this project started:

1. **Create a workspace.** This organizing process could take weeks or months depending on your photo collection. Ideally, use a large table where you can spread out your work and leave it undisturbed for an extended period.

2. **Gather.** Collect all photos you have throughout the house and bring them to your workspace.

3. **Designate a block of time to work.**

   - Use a timer and set it for 1- to 2-hour increments while you work to stay focused.

   - Schedule appointments on your calendar to continually revisit the project.

4. **Choose a storage option.** Photos can be stored in photo albums, boxes or a combination of both. The best way to store your printed photos is to use archival quality products. This means they should be free of acid and lignin. Check out www.archivalmethods.com or Amazon for supplies.

5. **Sort and Edit.** Go through your photos sorting them into three separate categories.

- BEST. These are photos that truly look good. Let go of duplicates or mail to friends or family. Collect enough photos that provide a complete representation of the event. (Storing these photos in an album will allow you to easily enjoy them.)

- GOOD. These photos will be of lesser quality than the BEST photos but they are important to you. Perhaps they tell a story that is not captured in any other photo. (While they may not be album worthy, these photos can be stored in a photo safe box.)

- BAD. Photos that should be tossed are those with poor exposure, heads cut off, bad view, etc. If you're a scrap booker, parts of these photos may be useful to you.

6. **Organize.** There are a few ways to organize your photos once they are sorted.

- Theme or event (i.e. weddings, birthdays, vacations, etc.)

- Chronologically. Be careful here, as this can be a stumbling block for some folks. Try not to get up hung up on capturing the exact date but rather group a few years together (i.e.1999–2002).

- Family member (i.e. Jimmy's Photo album)

Bonus:

- Do not use a ball point pen or permanent marker to write on the back of photos. Use a photo safe pencil to prevent damage. Check out: archivalmethods.com

- Do not use sticky notes on the front of your photos — the adhesive could damage your photo.

- Do not use plastic bags, envelopes or shoeboxes for long term storage as they will damage the integrity of the photo.

92. My aging parents are having difficulty keeping their medical information organized and in order. Any suggestions on how I may help them?

It's a challenge to keep up with medical documents since they may change each month with adjustments to medications or routines prescribed by doctors.

Help your parents create a personal health journal. Utilize a 3-ring binder filled with divider inserts. Include sections for health history, insurance information, medications, treatment diary, doctor visit Q&A and lab tests.

> **Bonus:** Smead makes an all-in-one healthcare and wellness file you can find on their website, myorganized.life.

93. Are there any papers I can throw out, without spending too much time thinking through them?

Yes!! We all have papers in our house that we may have collected and simply forgot to deal with. Here's a quick toss list for you:

- Expired coupons or store circulars
- Old greeting/birthday cards
- Invitations to events that have passed
- Outdated schedules
- Owner manuals for items you no longer possess
- Recipes you haven't tried in a year and thought you would
- Magazines older than a year
- Solicitations from charities you do not intend to support
- Old newspapers
- School papers from previous school year

94. How long should I keep bills?

Many people hang onto documents for fear of the consequences that may result when letting them go too soon. Here are general guidelines, if you have unusual circumstances or need further information please consult your attorney, accountant or visit www.irs.gov.

Keep forever:

- Marriage License
- Birth Certificates
- Wills
- Adoption Papers

- Death Certificates
- Social Security cards
- Insurance Policies

Keep tax documents...

The commonly referenced time period of "7 years" may not apply to you. Every situation is individual. Please check with your lawyer, accountant, and IRS (irs.gov).

Keep until reconciled

- ATM and deposit receipts
- Credit card receipts
- Bills — keep until the payment has been verified on the next bill.

Keep as long as you own the item

- Car titles and maintenance records
- Property records
- Warranty and user manuals (most of these can now be found online)

Bonus: Regarding utility bills, I suggest keeping the last statement for the year. If you sell your home, these bills are a useful reference to determine the average expenses associated with a home.

95. I would like to update the filing system in my home office. Do you have some general tips on what I should do?

In today's culture, we are bombarded with an endless stream of paper from various sources, which explains why it is the largest contributor to home/office clutter.

While there is no "one size fits all" paper management system, here are general tips to stay ahead of the paper train.

Begin by sorting and consolidating the paper you currently have into three categories. (Keep — Archive — Recycle/Shred)

- **Keep:** Current and active files.

  This needs to be information you use often enough that it is worthy of taking up prime real estate in your desk. Since most desks have only two file drawers, you need to be discriminating about what you will consider as active files. Some examples include: weekly reports, tax receipts for the current year, unpaid bills, projects in progress and school papers for the current year.

- **Archive:** Files needed for future reference.

  These are documents that you need to keep for reference but are not considered active. They can be stored elsewhere in your home or in your office but not in your desk as this space is reserved for active items only.

  Create an itemized inventory and include the specific location of all documents you place into **Archive** storage. In the event you need to locate a specific file you can do so with ease by referring to your inventory list. Store your inventory list on your computer and print a copy. Label it "Archive Inventory" and store it with your **Keep** files.

  Some examples of **Archive** items include: tax returns, product user manuals, mortgage documents, etc.

- **Recycle or Shred.** The last category is anything you no longer need to keep. Recycle when you can and shred anything with personal information. Documents with your name, address and any full or partial numbers related to your banking, finance and social security should be shredded.

96. How can I create a basic filing system for my home and home-based business?

Creating a filing system is the cornerstone to managing the flood of paper that crosses the threshold of our home. Without a filing system in place — the paper chaos ensues. Piles begin to form on flat surfaces throughout the house because nothing has a permanent designation. This is a step by step process to create a filing system that can cross multiple platforms — work, school, personal interest and household management.

1. Begin with a hanging file folder, labeled with a major category title. For example: Utilities. When it comes to labeling — I recommend a black sharpie marker for easy visibility or a label maker.

2. Use manila folders placed inside the hanging file folder labeled with sub-categories that relate to the major category. In the case of Utilities, you can have a sub-folder for gas, one for electric, trash and water. Now, any bill that comes into your house, once paid will have a place to live when you file it away.

You can also use this filing system for your children's school papers. The hanging file folder with a major category title will be labeled with your child's name. The sub-folders within the major file will be labeled with the various

> **Bonus:** Go paperless where possible and you'll have less to file away.

activities related to your child. For example, School Documents, Physicals, Soccer, Scouts, and Youth Group.

97. What is your favorite office organizing tool?

I love my label maker, but it's a close second to my paper shredder. This one tool can lend a hand in keeping up with the constant flow of paper that enters the home or office while protecting your identity. You can use a shredder to safely rid yourself of documents containing personal information when editing old files or sorting through daily mail.

> **Bonus:** Excessive amounts of paper to be shredded can be collected by a professional document company or you can take it to a UPS or Staples store near you for shredding.

DON'T SAY MISCELLANEOUS BUT...

Organizing experts will tell you...never label a drawer, file or box
"Miscellaneous."

Reason? Anything can fall into the category of miscellaneous and become
overloaded. Well, here I am, breaking the rules. This chapter contains
random questions that do not fall under a specific category. However, they
are each worthy of answering and had to be included in the book.

All that is not eternal is eternally useless.

∽ C.S. Lewis ∽

98. I used to be so organized. Can you explain how clutter happens?

The accumulation of clutter happens for different reasons.

- **Decisions.** You may have a difficult time making decisions about what you should keep or release so you put off making those choices and the clutter builds from here.

- **Value.** If you see something as valuable, even if it's no longer functioning or being used, you may hang onto it. Have you ever bought an expensive appliance that breaks; but instead of finding the time to fix it or simply let it go, you hang onto it because in your mind, letting it go equates to letting go of money?

- **"I might need it someday!"** You may not want to let go of something for fear that you will need it at some point in the eminent future.

- **Situational Clutter.** A circumstance or life situation causes a sudden influx of excess into our space. A death of a loved one, a child returns home or an unexpected move causes us to downsize our home. The situation brings along unexpected papers, memorabilia, clothes and possessions.

- **Shopping Habits.** Sales, BOGO's, and coupons, oh my! It's not uncommon that clutter is linked to shopping habits. If someone is motivated to shop for anything based on a sale price rather than a genuine need, then it's quite easy to acquire clutter.

- **Free Stuff.** Some folks are drawn to anything that's free. Even if they don't need it. Hand-me-downs fall into this category as well. Once these items are brought into the house, they may never leave. I'm not suggesting you decline the offer of gently used items from friends or family. What I am recommending is you make a choice, to keep or not keep items based on need and then donate the rest.

Simplicity is the ultimate sophistication.

&ᴠ Leonardo Di Vinci ᴠ

---

99. I keep hearing more and more about minimalism. What is it exactly?

Webster's dictionary defines minimalism as a style or technique (as in music, literature, or design) that is characterized by extreme sparseness and simplicity.

Joshua Becker began an entire movement with his own exploration and journey into minimalism. Here is his definition which I like:

> *Minimalism is the intentional promotion of the things we most value and the removal of everything that distracts us from it. It is a life that forces intentionality. And as a result, it forces improvements in almost all aspects of your life.*

In my experience, many people are fearful of the idea of minimalism because in their minds it means giving up everything. I recommend a compromise with what I like to call **modified minimalism**. Taking steps to remove the excess while still keeping what you enjoy. Once we begin the release process in one area of our home or life, there tends to be a gradual shift in the way we think and how we want to live moving forward. In the end, the release of any excess is based on creating the life that you and your family are most comfortable with.

100. I am always losing my keys! What can I do to prevent this from happening?

House and car keys are small objects that can easily get misplaced or forgotten. One of these ideas should help:

- Designate a permanent home for your keys and stick to it. Perhaps a decorative bowl or hook near your home's entryway.

- Attach your keys to a carabiner latch (available at hardware stores) and hook them onto your purse strap or belt loop.

- Use an electronic device to help you quickly locate lost keys or anything else. Tile (thetileapp.com) or TrackR (secure.thetrackr.com) are two such devices.

- Last thought: if you have an attached garage, leave the keys in your car's console or cup holder. You'll have one less thing to think about and your keys will always be waiting for you when you depart.

101. I am tired of digging through my purse to find my lipstick, phone, a pen or whatever. Should I consider a smaller purse or carry less stuff?

Neither!!

On Amazon.com you can find a variety of purse organizing inserts. Choose a style you like best. This pouch fits into any handbag or diaper bag. The insert has over a dozen small compartments to keep every little thing in its place. Put the purse organizer inside the handbag of your choice, fill and go. It's wonderful for folks who change handbags frequently-just lift the insert from one handbag and transfer to another.

Remember, an occasional edit of your purse is a good idea.

102. I found these pretty decorative boxes that have inspired me to organize my office. What else should I buy before I get started?

I'm glad you've decided to organize your office. However, try not to fall prey to a common organizing pitfall: buying shiny, pretty organizing products before you are actually organized.

The first step in any organizing process is to edit the contents of your space. Once you've decided what to keep you can choose the right size container for storage, as well as determine what other tools you may need.

Before you head to the store, take measurements of your spaces to get the right size containers. Keep your receipts until you are certain this storage system is working for you.

103. A new job has made life suddenly so hectic. Any ideas on how to simplify my life?

A busy, non-stop life can weigh you down physically, mentally and spiritually.

Here is a list of small steps you can use to guide you on the road to simplicity.

1) Let go of the idea that everything has to be perfect. Done is better than none.

2) Set up bill payments online to decrease the flow of mail.

3) Keep a stash of blank notecards on hand. These cards can work for any occasion and save you a trip to the store.

4) Bathroom cleanups are easier if you keep some cleaning supplies under the sink cabinet of each bathroom.

5) Enclose necessary coupons and gift cards in an envelope and use the front of the envelope as your shopping list.

6) Sort through your mail on a daily basis.

7) Reclaim some kitchen cabinet or counter space by donating those rarely used gadgets like coffee grinder, bread maker, food sealer, etc.

8) Limit your decorative knickknacks throughout the house to help making dusting your house much easier.

9) Cancel or do not renew subscriptions to magazines that you can't keep up with reading.

10) Rather than purchase an item you rarely use; can you borrow it from someone instead?

11) Go through your clothes each season and donate items you have not worn in the last year.

12) Wipe down shelves in the refrigerator before you grocery shop.

13) When planning your day, avoid scheduling every minute, leave some open time just in case you're running behind or you want to take a moment to pause.

14) When you use something, put it back where it belongs.

15) Schedule time for yourself. Write it on your calendar and treat that time like any other appointment.

16) Pack non-perishables in your and your child's lunch boxes the night before.

17) Stop unnecessary volunteering and do not feel guilty about it.

18) At the end of each day, create a "to do" list for tomorrow.

19) Learn to delegate some responsibilities, this will free up your time to do something else.

20) Take a day off each week from using anything electronic-read a book or go for a walk.

Everything in excess is opposed to nature.

ॐ Hippocrates ॐ

104. Do insurance companies require documentation of household items in the event of a man-made or natural disaster?

It is not a requirement, but to settle a claim for losses faster it certainly helps. You will also be more likely to get a higher value for your belongings with appropriate documentation. This pro-active protection is a good idea against claims of theft, as well.

Here's how you can do your own home inventory:

- Walking from room to room, list all of your furniture and possessions. Include valuables from cabinets and drawers.

- Describe each item, include purchase price, model and serial numbers if possible.

- If you have sales receipts, they should be included in your documentation as well.

- Back up your written inventory list and photos electronically in your computer.

- You can choose to take the digital route which can save you the extra step of recording items manually. There are several inventory apps such as Allstate Digital Locker, Sortly and Liberty Mutual Home Gallery that can streamline the process for you.

105. My sister's overbuying is leading to more and more clutter in her tiny apartment. Any advice to help her stop spending?

Mindless shopping habits can easily lead to clutter.

Before a purchase is made, your sister could ask herself these qualifying questions:

- **Do I really need it?** Examine the need for the purchase carefully before putting it in your cart.

- **Do I have anything else like it at home?** Clutter and disorganization can prevent folks from seeing what they may already have in their possession.

- **Do I know someone that already owns this item**? It's better to borrow than to buy, especially if it's an item that you would use infrequently.

- **If I do buy this item, what kind of maintenance will be required?** This could be the deal breaker, so read the label. Many folks end up with stuff in their house they never use because of maintenance issues that went unchecked.

- **If the item is on sale...is that the only reason I'm buying it?** A sale should not be the sole reason a purchase is made. A genuine need should be present.

Bonus: More practical shopping advice:

- **Shop with intention**. Use a list of what you need rather than succumb to impulse buying.

- **Choose quality over quantity**. Two pairs of well-made jeans are better than eight pairs of lesser, inferior brands.

- ***One-in-one-out* rule**. If you plan to bring it home, plan to let something else go.

106. Do you think it's necessary to stock pile supplies for a potential disaster?

September is National Preparedness Month and I always use that time of year to remind folks that a disaster (natural or man-made) can strike. It's a good idea to have a plan of action and supplies in place. Authorities such as the Red Cross suggest keeping enough supplies to last 72 hours.

Here's what you'll need to create what I like to call, a "Grab-n-Go" tote:

- Begin by using a heavy-duty tote with lid (you may need 2–4 depending on the size of your family). Using tape, mark the pack date on the lid of your tote so you can refresh packed items with expiration dates, as needed.

- A complete change of clothing for each family member.

- Mess kits — these are all-in-one cooking, eating and utensil kits used in outdoor camping.

- First Aid kit.

- Matches, flashlights and batteries.

- Non-perishable, high protein foods (peanut butter, protein bars, whole grain cereal, crackers, nuts).

- Battery operated radio (leave batteries out of the radio until ready to use).

- Manual can opener.

- Canned pet food if you have a dog or cat.

- Baby formula, if applicable.

- One gallon of water per person/day. Water for pets too.

- Toiletries such as toothpaste, tooth brushes, toilet paper, deodorant, and hand soap.

- Store copies of hard to replace documents inside a secure plastic bag inside your tote. If you need to evacuate your home quickly, items such as birth certificates, social security cards, passports, home inventory lists, financial documents and some cash will be helpful to have with you.

- Write up an evacuation plan in the event your family is not together or reachable by phone when disaster strikes. Plans should include a meeting spot, maps, phone numbers etc. Review plans with your family and store written plans in the glove compartment of each family vehicle.

- Include a note in or on top of the tote with some final reminders such as: bring your pet(s), sleeping bags and prescription medications.

107. I have been cleaning out our attic and basement and have unusual items to donate or recycle but I'm not sure where they should go.

I applaud you for taking the initiative to dispose of your unwanted goods in a responsible way.

Below is a list of some common hard to recycle items.

- **Electronic devices** — computers, cell phones and televisions can be dropped off at Best Buy stores for recycling. Be sure to consult with a computer expert who can wipe your devices of any residual data before you recycle them.

- **Crutches, walkers or wheelchairs** — Your local Goodwill donation center. Western PA residents can also donate to Global Links (globallinks.org) who will accept medical supplies and shares them worldwide with those in need.

- **Paint** — Home Depot sells a paint hardener or you can use cat litter to dry any paint that remains in a can. Once the paint completely hardens you can throw it in the trash. If you have mostly full cans of paint, Habitat for Humanity (habitat.org) could use them.

- **Eyeglasses** — Lions Club International (lionsclub.org) and New Eyes Vision (new-eyes.org) will allow you to mail in your glasses for recycling.

- **Furniture pickup** — Vietnam Vets (pickupplease.org), Habitat for Humanity (habitat.org), Salvation Army (satruck.org), and your local Goodwill Industries (goodwill.org). Check respective websites for qualifications on furniture.

- **Building supplies** — Check your area for a Habitat for Humanity location.

- **Mattresses** — If you're local to Western Pennsylvania, reach out to Off the Floor (offthefloor.org) or Who's your Brother (whosyourbrother.org).

Check with your local authorities to see if they are planning a recycling day for hard-to-dispose of items. These community recycle days are easier to find as responsible recycling becomes the norm in today's culture.

108. What does hoarding really look like?

According to the dictionary, to hoard is simply to save or accumulate stuff. In organizing and medical circles, the term takes on a deeper meaning. In the most recent edition of the Diagnostic and Statistical Manual of Mental Disorders (DSM-5), hoarding is classified as a mental disorder. Someone with hoarding tendencies excessively saves items and the idea of discarding the items causes extreme distress.

The Learning Channel features a program entitled, *Hoarding: Buried Alive*. Each episode follows a participant through the process of assessment, therapy and eventual clean out of their home and surrounding property. The program has shed light on an issue that was rarely seen in the public eye. Despite all of the media attention, only 2%–5% of people fit the criteria for hoarding.

According to the Institute for Challenging Disorganization (ICD) (challengingdisorganization.org), an organization dedicated to educating the public and professionals in the area of chronic disorganization and hoarding is characterized by:

1) The acquisition of, and failure to discard possessions that appear to be useless or of limited value.

2) Living spaces are sufficiently cluttered as to preclude their intended use.

3) Significant distress is caused by the clutter.

To further explain the assessment of hoarding tendencies, the ICD has created a free document available from their website known as the Clutter Hoarding Scale. This scale is an assessment tool to determine the health and safety needs of those working in a residential environment. It is not intended to classify people, only the environment. The scale consists of 5 levels. Here is a brief synopsis of each level:

Level I is standard living, common disorganization.

Level II clutter is affecting some functions of the living space. Some household appliances are not fully functioning. Slight congestion to exits and hallways. Inconsistent routine of housekeeping.

Level III is the shift change between a cluttered home and a hoarding environment. In addition to the evidence from a Level II home, there will be at least one room not being used for its intended purpose.

Sanitation and hazardous conditions are more of a health concern for occupants of the home.

Level IV Some visual markers include clutter spilling over to the outside of the home and within vehicles. Reduced accessibility and use of key living areas. Inappropriate use of appliances. Mold and mildew are present. Clutter blocks access to hallways and exits. Mental health professionals, cleaning contractors and professional organizers would be essential to the cleanup effort.

Level V is what is commonly seen on the program, *"Hoarding: Buried Alive."* These individuals are living in unsafe conditions with most of their living spaces being unusable. Health and safety concerns force the homeowner to take action. Assistance must come in the form of a collaborative team of service providers including professional organizers, mental health professionals, cleaning contractors, social workers and animal control.

Have nothing in your house that you do not know to be useful, or believe to be beautiful.

&ntp; William Morris ❧

109. I want to help my roommate understand the real cost of clutter. Can you help me explain?

Many of us can adjust and adapt to excess clutter but at what cost? Let's explore the tangible and intangible issues that arise from having too much stuff.

Clutter can cost you time:

- There is time lost looking for misplaced items.

- Meals take more time to prepare in a disorganized kitchen.

- A cluttered closet means more time to decide what to wear.

- The distractions of clutter can cause a slow-down in productivity.

Clutter can cost you money:

- Misplaced or lost bills can incur late fees.

- Buying duplicate items you already own but cannot find.

- Are you missing an opportunity for advancement at work?

  According to CareerBuilder.com, 28% of employers say they are less likely to promote someone who has a disorganized desk.[17]

- Are you renting storage space to hold your excess belongings? Think of the expense this is adding to your monthly budget.

- In the workplace, lost time searching for anything means lost revenue.

Clutter can cost you your health:

- A cluttered living or workspace can make it difficult to clean which can create an accumulation of dust and allergens.

- The visual appearance of clutter is a drain on your brain and energy level, which can lead to increased stress and anxiety.

- Feelings of embarrassment that may arise from having friends over or not being able to have them over because of the clutter.

I hope these considerations will motivate your roommate to remove the excess clutter in his/her life.

110. Can you please share some quick clutter clearing tips to help me start somewhere?

When you have a large space to work on, it can be overwhelming to think about doing it all at once. Here are ten baby steps to get you started:

1) Take any large project and break it down into smaller tasks.

2) Even ten minutes of organizing can make an impact. Work on one drawer or one shelf.

3) Stop putting off the task because you strive for perfection. Be happy with each small success, as it is a step in the right direction.

4) Enlist a friend or professional organizer to hold you accountable to get the work done.

5) Nearly all de-cluttering begins with sorting items into the following categories:

- Keep
- Donate
- Trash/ recycle

6) Start incorporating the *one-in-one-out* rule for everything. If you buy something new, release an item from the same category

7) Shop for storage containers <u>after</u> you've sorted and edited your space.

8) Stop the clutter at the checkout counter. Before you purchase an item, ask yourself these questions:

- Do I really need it at all?
- Can I borrow it from someone?
- Do I have room for this new purchase?

9) Create a place for everything in your home.

10) If you can't tidy up after yourself immediately, then spend 10–15 minutes a day to keep up with it.

- Eat a meal — put away your dishes.
- Bring in the mail —sort it out.
- Change clothes — put them back on the hanger.

Every little bit helps and everyone in the house can help.

111. Spring time means cleaning my whole house and that is overwhelming to me.

This deep cleaning ritual is not limited to being performed in the spring. It may seem less overwhelming if you view it as a 3- to 6-month process that you can do in small steps. Do what you can each day and it will eventually get done.

Home Office

- Release older documents or move them into archive files to free up active file space.

- Review magazines and catalogs. Use magazine holders to store your favorites and consider canceling subscriptions if you are not reading them.

- Dust surfaces and wipe or wash window treatments.

Kitchen

- Clear out the refrigerator, freezer and pantry of old, unused or unwanted goods.

- Have you acquired an excess of kitchen towels, dishcloths and rags? Keep enough to fit in one drawer.

- How about those gadgets, appliances and tools that you thought were going to be the next best thing? If you do not use them, then you do not need to keep them or continue to clean them.

- Take a peak in your junk drawer and toss out unnecessary multiples and relocate items that do not belong but somehow manage to find their way into that drawer.

- Wipe down cabinet doors and all surface areas.

Family Gathering Room

- Edit VHS tapes, DVD's, books and games. Donate these to local libraries, schools and churches.

- Dust all surfaces and clean window treatments.

Play Spaces

- Sort through toys, videos and gaming items. If your kids have outgrown something or lost interest in a toy, donate to your favorite charity.

- Clean surfaces and wipe down toys.

Bathrooms

- Check your medicine cabinet, and first aid kit. Recycle expired medication and unused prescriptions. Check the Drug Enforcement Agency website (deadiversion.usdoj.gov) for the National Drug Take Back day. Most municipalities will institute a drug collection program in conjunction with the national date. Turn in your expired medications on this Take Back day for proper disposal. You can also check with your pharmacy.

- Don't forget your makeup bag. Beauty experts suggest keeping makeup no longer than 6 months to avoid bacteria build up. Toss out old products and purchase new ones.

Closets

- Take a closer look at your clothes, shoes and apparel accessories. Determine what has not been worn in the last year and why. Do you really need it? Does it look good on you? Can it serve someone else who will wear it more regularly? Donate items you no longer wear to your favorite charity.

- Dust off hangers, hat boxes and flat surfaces.

While carrying out your spring-cleaning objectives, I encourage you to take the time to edit your belongings throughout the house. Ultimately, the less you own, the less there will be to clean.

112. My parents are moving from a 3,200 square foot house to a 1,600 square foot patio home. Do you have any tips for their downsizing?

Downsizing is a common trend these days due to retirement, empty nesters looking to live in a smaller home or an increase in living expenses.

Keep these thoughts in mind to help you and your parents get through the downsizing process:

- Don't wait until the existing house is sold to begin your work. The earlier you begin the less rushed your parents will feel in their decision-making.

- Take a physical assessment of the new living space, especially storage areas. Drawing comparisons to the current space can assist your parents in discerning what's most important to keep.

- Sort and Edit. Go through all possessions, room by room and sort into 4 categories:

  - Keep

  - Donate

  - Give to a family member or friend

  - Trash

- Recruit family members to help. Be mindful to focus on the task at hand as reminiscing through mementos can get you off-course and you could lose precious work time.

- To save time and your sanity, consider an estate sale to clear out large quantities of possessions you do not plan to move.

- Be positive and patient. The entire process can bring on a mix of emotions for everyone in the family. Visit the National Association of Senior Move Managers website (nasmm.org) for more information and resources.

113. What is your favorite top tip?

My favorite tip is repurposing a closet. It's often a space that most homeowners would not think to alter but can make a transformational difference in acquiring functional space where there was none.

Closets can change from a place of storage to a resourceful area such as a craft room, play space, office, sewing room, reading nook, and more. You can leave the closet doors on or off, add shelves, a desktop, cabinets, storage cubbies and anything else required to fulfill your goals for the space.

Check out the ATO Pinterest board for a few inspiring examples.

114. Is there a link between clutter and ADHD?

ADHD (Attention Deficit Hyperactivity Disorder) is a medical condition that is often first identified in school age children. Some symptoms include the inability to focus, sit still and impulsive behavior.

Dr. Melva Green, a psychiatrist who frequently appears on the television program, Hoarders, says "Many, many hoarders have ADHD, and all with ADHD are at risk of becoming hoarders."

These are solutions I utilize to control the clutter.

- Spend 15 minutes each day doing some decluttering in any part of your home.

- Keep a waste basket in every room and use it.

- Use storage containers without lids. A simple toss in the container is easier than the extra step of lifting off a lid.

- Live by the *one-in-one-out* rule with everything. For example, magazines, when the new issue arrives, let go of the last issue.

- Create a collection or junk drawer for each room. Fill it with those random items so they do not collect on surfaces. When the drawer is full, take the time to empty it out and make decisions about what should stay or go.

- Sort through mail and papers coming into the home each day.

- Create a simple filing system as mentioned in question #96.

Space is the breath of art.

&? Frank Lloyd Wright &?

---

115. I'm going on a mission trip for 2 weeks and can only bring one bag. Do you have advice to help me pack efficiently?

When packing for a trip, you will need to consider what you're packing and choose a method that will allow you to bring what you need while still keeping your clothes from getting wrinkled.

- **Rolling your items** like a burrito allows you to fit more into a bag rather than traditional folding.

- **Bundle.** If you're packing nicer clothes you may want to consider the bundle method. Lay down the piece of clothing most prone to wrinkles. Top that piece with 3–4 more pieces of clothing and give the whole pile a fold on each side so it becomes a neat square. The idea here is that the outermost piece will have the least number of wrinkles.

- **Use Compression Bags.** These bags are specially designed for packing. Put your clothes in the bag and seal. Roll out the extra air and place in your suitcase.

Use one or a combination of the above-mentioned techniques in order to accommodate the various types of clothes you may be packing.

116. Do you have any suggestions for packing and organizing for a vacation so it's less stressful for me?

Prepare: Enjoying your vacation begins by not worrying about anything at home. Visit my website organizationlane.com under the Resources tab is a free, printable checklist on what to do before you leave for vacation.

Plan: Research the weather and plan your outfits accordingly. Bring neutrals or complimentary colors so you can mix and match. Wear an outer layer on the plane rather than pack it and take up a large amount of space in your suitcase.

Pack:

- If you think you will be bringing home more stuff than when you left, pack a light tote under the liner of your suitcase or pack a small suitcase and place it inside a larger suitcase. That way you only have to pay for one checked bag (at least on the trip out).

- Don't fold, roll. Use packing cubes to organize or compression bags to maximize the space in your luggage.

- Use your packed shoes as storage. Fill them with undergarments, socks and rolled pajamas.

- Socks can be used to store small, fragile items such as a perfume or an essential oil bottle.

- Keep your charger in your carry-on bag. If you encounter any delays, you don't want to run out of battery life.

- Ditch the full-size products and use trial size options. A contact lens case can store just the right amount of concealer and/or moisturizer.

- Use an eye glass case or pencil bag for jewelry.

- Lighten your suitcase by wearing your heaviest shoes or outerwear on travel day.

Snacks: Pack snacks for yourself and kids. Whether you are traveling by car or plane — you never know what delays may interfere with your plans. Avoid getting "hangry" with power bars, packages of trail mix, ready to eat tuna packets.

Cut back on Souvenirs: Be selective about what you bring home. Remember it may most likely end up on a tag sale table in a few years. Cut down on the clutter and let your photos be the only mementos you keep.

A few extra tips:

- Full bottles of water will get confiscated at security. Bring an empty water bottle to the airport. You can fill it up when you get beyond the security checkpoint (many airports have bottle filling stations).

- Take pictures of important travel docs — passport and itineraries. Store in the photo library of your smartphone so you can access them off line if necessary.

- If you forget your smart phone wall charger brick — don't buy one — plug your charging cord into the USB port of the flat screen tv in your hotel room located on the backside of the screen.

117. Our hat/mitten storage is in one huge basket in our closet and it's not working. Please share a helpful hint for us?

The larger the family, the more hats/gloves you will have and finding a storage solution to keep it all organized and kid-friendly is not always an easy task.

Depending on your closet configuration, here are a few ideas that may work:

- Edit your contents. How many do you use and need? Does every glove have a match? If not, toss it.

- Use small baskets or bins and designate one for each family member which will help reduce the search time for an item. Label each basket so there is no confusion as to where items should be returned. These bins may sit on a shelf or find stackable bins that can fit on the floor of your closet.

- To keep gloves together fold them as a pair, just as you might with a pair of socks.

- An over-the-door clear pocket shoe organizer is another option. You can choose to label each pocket with its contents or assign a certain number of pockets to each family member. Assign the lower pockets for your children so they can easily reach their own items. The pockets are just the right size for gloves, a folded hat, scarf or sunglasses.

118. I'm having a hard time letting go of sentimental items. I need to do something because we're moving from a house to an apartment and I can't take it all with me. How do I get passed the guilt?

Sentimental items and family heirlooms can bring up a wave of emotions: happiness, sadness, guilt and anxiety. Consider these thoughts to ease you through the process:

- **Set limits.** Designate a small to medium size keepsake box to collect your sentimental items and limit your collection to this one box. This will require you to be mindful and selective about what you keep.

- **Take a picture and tell a story.** Digitize your sentimental items with a photo. Be sure to include the story that goes along with the item. This option preserves family memories without keeping the object itself.

- **Share.** There may be other family members who are interested in adopting the keepsakes. Make a call to see if someone else has the space or interest in being the family archivist.

- **Let go of the bad juju.** Say goodbye to possessions with a negative history. For example, a client of mine had several awards and plaques from an old job. A job he did for 18 years, however, the company let him go. With his tenure ending on a bad note, these awards were no longer positive accolades to him, they were adverse tokens that he would rather soon forgot.

- **In the end, it's just stuff.** Remember, it's the memory or the person associated with the memory that is meaningful not the physical stuff.

119. What statistics can you tell me about the organizing industry?

These statistics serve as daily reminders to me of the clutter that consumes our society today.

- The size of the American home has doubled since the 1950's.

- Despite the extra square footage in homes, 1 in every 10 households will rent a storage unit to store their excess stuff.

- There are over 50,000 storage facilities across the US.

- There are 300,000 items in the average American home.

- The US has less than 4% of the world's children but we purchase 40% of the world's toys.

- Shopping malls outnumber high schools.

- Americans spend more on shoes, jewelry and watches than higher education.

- US Department of Energy reports that one-quarter of people with two-car garages have so much stuff in there that they can't park a car.

- Harris Interactive reports, 23% of adults say they pay bills late (and incur fees) because they lose them.

- Stephanie Wilson, author of The Organized Executive, estimates that mangers lose one hour/day due to disorder.

- In the US, television sets outnumber the people in a home.

- Women will spend more than 8 years of their life shopping.

120. Your house must always be perfectly organized, right?

Over the years, I have noticed that people have certain expectations of me because of what I do which led me to write this confessional article years ago.

Confessions of an Organizer

Confession #1 — Time Management

I have been late to a doctor's appointment, a meeting and a party. Each time I was late, it reinforced what I already knew. The tardiness came from poor planning. I review my schedule each night in preparation for the next day. I have also become mindful not to over-schedule myself or my kids and I build in extra time for the unexpected.

Confession #2 — Clutter Control

My family and I accumulate clutter. Whether it's clothes, books, electronics, etc. It happens in every house. The important thing is to recognize it and be proactive. I've found the best defense is to have an on-going bag for donations and load it as needed. When the bag is full, I'll make a trip to donate them.

Confession #3 — Pass it On

Being a professional organizer does not mean my kids are perfectly organized. Organization is like any other habit. It may take years before you see glimpses of the habits you are trying to pass onto your kids. When I originally wrote this newspaper column, my kids where in middle and high school. They are both in college now and I clearly see them using organizational skills I thought went in one ear and out the other. Never give up, your kids are listening, watching and learning.

Confession #4 — The Closet of Shame

Every once in a while, my closet or a drawer will transform into a jumbled mess. Ideally, I know I should take the time to put clothes away neatly as I disrobe. However, life can get in the way, so the next best solution is to make the time to straighten it out. I set aside 10–15 minutes in the evening to get caught up and organize the disorder and I always feel so much better.

Confession #5 — Perfectionism

Being an organizer does not make me perfect. I strive to do my best and I'm perfectly happy with that.

121. How do I become a professional organizer?

Begin by visiting your local NAPO (National Association of Productivity and Organizing Professionals) chapter. Meetings are held monthly and a small guest fee is usually required. This will give you a sense of the business and connect you with fellow organizers in your area. You can locate a chapter near you by visiting: www.napo.net

You may want to start out small by performing sub-contract work for an established organizer. This will give you a real taste of what it's like to be in the field communicating and working with clients.

I would then recommend joining NAPO at the national level and then the chapter level. Your national membership begins as a Provisional member. During this provisional period, you can take some educational courses that will help get your organizing career off to a solid start. Membership benefits include networking, education, volunteer opportunities, credibility, camaraderie and endless industry resources.

You can work for an organizer already in business or open your own business. If you decide on the latter, I encourage you to take a basic business course. I also recommend reading *From Start-Up to Success* by Melanie Colusci (Amazon.com). This book is an easy read to help any entrepreneur get their business off the ground.

HOLIDAYS

Several years ago, my husband and I opted to forgo gift giving and used those designated funds to give our family the gift of a vacation. We went on a 4-day/3-night cruise to the Bahamas. My kids said it was the best Christmas they ever had. Sometimes, one decision can make life so simple and yet be so impactful.

When in doubt, choose simple, especially around the holidays which can leave many of us in a frenzied state.

I make myself rich by making my wants few.

∾ Henry David Thoreau ∾

122. I want to have a holiday party. Is there a way to entertain without getting riddled with anxiety?

The holidays are approaching and tis' the season for entertaining. Whether you are having a small dinner party or hosting a gathering of 20+ you can reduce your stress and have fun with your guests by doing some advanced planning.

Here's a step-by-step plan for hosting any event:

1. **Select the date of your event.** Check your calendar for some free dates and reach out to your guests. There are various ways to invite guests: electronic invitations (Evite.com), a personal phone call, email or traditional paper invitation. The important thing to remember is to give yourself the time you need to create and send your invites.

2. **Create a menu for your event.** These days, guests enjoy contributing something to the meal. If you are short on time, take them up on their offer. First decide what you will prepare and have your guests fill the gaps in your menu by suggesting items that will complement each other.

3. **Keep your dishes simple.** This is not the time to try out Martha Stewart's 16 ingredient, flambé sweet potato surprise for the first time. New recipes can add to your stress so stick with dishes you've made before.

4. **Write up your shopping list.** Gather your recipes together and check your supplies in order to create your shopping list. Don't forget to check beverage items as well. If you're serving mixed drinks include any extras such as olives, limes, cherries, etc. Be sure to have disposable plastic containers for any leftovers you may send home with guests.

   To reduce some running around, set up your shopping list according to the layout of the store.

5. **Take an inventory** of any other items for your table setting such as linens, centerpiece, candles, etc. and add them to your list. Refrain from buying anything new just for the event. See if you can borrow the item you need from a friend. Case in point, years ago I had a formal dinner party and wanted to serve coffee out of a decorative electric urn and not my little Mr. Coffee brewer. Instead

of buying one, I borrowed an urn from a friend who was so happy to loan it to me since the urn was underutilized.

6. **Check your calendar** and plan which day(s) you will shop. Take into consideration that you may need to go to more than one store and some items may need to be purchased closer to the event date such a flowers or fresh vegetables. **Be sure to keep the day before your event open for anything you may have missed on your list.**

7. **Select the dishes that can be made in advance** so you do not have to make everything on the day of the event.

8. **Cue up the music.** Have a playlist of music ready to go so you can simply hit 'play' when the doorbell rings.

9. The day before your event, **set your table**. Pull out your serving platters, utensils, and create your centerpiece.

10. **Clear out your closet** of coats to make room for your guest's outerwear.

With a plan in place you can enjoy your party and perhaps you'll do it more often.

123. Help!! It's December 16 and I'm so far from ready for the holidays, how can I catch up?

Kids, work, volunteerism, caregiving, etc. are just a few reasons why families are so busy today. When you add the long list of tasks that are typically expected during this season such as decorating, cookies, party hosting, cards, shopping and wrapping, it's no wonder you can't keep up.

At this late juncture and given the pressure you may be under I am going to recommend ACCEPTANCE. Evaluate how your life has changed and why you are so busy. Accept those changes and the idea that doing a little less to celebrate the holiday will help you enjoy it more with your family.

Take a step back and see where you can cut back. For example, bake two kinds of cookies instead of eight different varieties. Another example is to skip decorating every room in your house and be content with getting your tree decorated.

124. Getting a family photo for a holiday card wears me out. How can I make it less stressful for all of us?

As if the holidays were not stressful enough, right? These ideas should make it easy for you to get that holiday card ready with time to spare.

- It's not usually on our minds but Thanksgiving is a great time to capture that perfect family picture for your holiday card. Everyone is already dressed up and there are plenty of people around to take your picture. I also suggest going through photos you've taken during the year. You may have an amazing picture already waiting for you.

- Create address labels on your computer and print them out. This not only saves time, it will be easy to update for next year's list.

- Recruit your kids to help stuff, seal and label your envelopes. Put on some holiday music and make it a family tradition.

> **Bonus:** Can't get your card out in time for Christmas? No worries, send a Happy New Year card instead. After the holiday hype is over you may have more time and your card will be a pleasant surprise in a mailbox full of Christmas bills.

125. We are having family and friends stay with us during the holiday season. Any suggestions on how I can prepare for their visits?

With a little advance preparation, you will be able to relax and enjoy the holiday with your family and any visiting guests.

Whether your guests are spending one night or having an extended stay, here are a few tips to consider:

- **Stock up on their favorite snacks and beverages.** Do a little bit of recon work and find out what your guests like to drink in their coffee. If there is a picky eater in the bunch, be sure to have something they like to eat. In general, a complete restocking of your pantry is a good idea.

- **Make room in your entryway closet.** Even if you are only hosting dinner guests make room in your entry closet to accommodate the extra coats and jackets.

119

- **Spare set of sheets and towels for guests only.** Keep a set of sheets and towels exclusively for guests so there is never any doubt that you have clean supplies on hand.

> **Bonus:** If your guests are sharing a bathroom with your family members, a set of different colored towels for guests can help avoid the confusion.

- **Prepare the bed in advance.** If space permits or if you have a guest bedroom, it's a good idea to make the bed ahead of time with freshly laundered sheets. The last thing you want to do after a late night with a tired guest is to scramble around looking for sheets.

- **Offer the comforts of home.** Stock your guest room with magazines, a couple of books, bottles of water, phone charging space, and toiletries.

- **Don't have a spare bedroom?** If you need some extra sleep space in your home, an inflatable mattress is a great investment and sets up in a matter of a minutes. (Available at most retailers)

- **Plan some fun things to do.** To help your visitors enjoy their stay, look into any special exhibits, shopping or concerts they may enjoy.

- **Clear out some drawer space.** Create some space in drawers or closets so your guests do not have to live out of their suitcase during their stay.

- **Prepare meals ahead.** When feeding the masses nothing beats some easy crock-pot or casserole recipes. Making your meals ahead and freezing them allows you to spend time with your guests rather than working in the kitchen. You can always order out too ;).

126. What suggestions do you have to not over-indulge with gift-giving?

My husband and I have found that limits on gift-giving bring simplicity into our home and prompt us to make more thoughtful decisions with our gifts.

I first read about the 4-gift rule several years ago. Our family has adopted this concept with open arms and we have not looked back.

At Christmas, each of our children receives four gifts:

- something they want
- something they need
- something to wear
- something to read

These limitations bring purpose and focus to your choices.

127. I feel like we have no room to store the new gifts we just received at Hanukah. How can I fit it all in our house?

If your family was blessed with an abundance of gifts, take a look at what you currently have on hand. Donate unused or no longer needed items to make room.

Use the *one-in-one-out* rule and apply it to everything: toys, books, movies, clothes, gadgets, gift bags/boxes and more. If one item comes in, then one should leave.

We make a living by what we get,
but we make a life by what we give.

&ampersand; Winston Churchill &ampersand;

---

128. Do you have any gift suggestions that do not create clutter?

Gift giving is enjoyed by nearly everyone throughout the year. I encourage folks to consider gifts that are thoughtful yet sensible.

Here are 20 ideas to help you be a clutter-free gift giver:

1) A year-long subscription to the zoo, museum, aviary or science center.

2) A good wine or a special micro-brew beer. For a larger gift, consider a year-long sampling.

3) For the coffee drinker — a specialty coffee, gift card or free refill card to their favorite coffee shop.

4) Fuel gift card or auto emergency kit for the student traveler.

5) Point of interest classes or workshops such as dancing, cooking, quilting, photography, etc.

6) There are hundreds of recipes for edible and drinkable treats which can be assembled inside a jar such as cookies, soups, stews and hot cocoa. Do an online search for 'recipes in a jar' and take your pick.

7) A visit to an indoor water park is a nice treat for the whole family especially in the dead of winter.

8) A gift certificate for fitness — Yoga, Pilates or any fitness center.

9) A gift card to a favorite store or restaurant. Consider local establishments when possible.

10) Instead of a hard cover book or CD — choose an e-book or iTunes gift card.

11) For the avid cook, specialty spices, oils or vinegars.

12) A charity or mission donation in someone's name.

13) A gift certificate for a therapeutic massage, hair or nail salon is a luxurious treat.

14) Movie, symphony, theatre, concert or sporting event tickets.

15) A gift certificate for a home/yard cleaning.

16) Homemade edible treats with an accompanying recipe to share.

17) For the couple with children, a free night of babysitting would be appreciated.

18) Hobby gifts — golfers, cyclers, crafters, scrap bookers and knitters would love supplies or a gift card from their favorite resource store.

19) For family members — a photo calendar filled with family pictures, birth dates and anniversaries.

20) The gift of time — home-made coupons for a family night of games and home movies is time well spent and will not cost you a penny.

Enjoy this season knowing that the right gift is out there and it probably does not need any dusting at all.

No one became poor by giving.

ʚ Anne Frank ɞ

129. What should I do with the Christmas cards we received this year? I always feel guilty tossing them in the trash so I keep them from year to year.

Despite our digital connections and photo sharing through Facebook and other media sites, cards are sent to extend sentiments of good cheer. What to do with these cards after the holiday can be a dilemma. Here are my ideas to thoughtfully repurpose your greeting and photo cards which can also be seen on the ATO Pinterest board:

- **Photos on a ring.** If you have photo cards, create a holiday card collection which will keep them organized and easy to view for years.
  - o Sort through the photo cards and keep those that are meaningful to you and your family.
  - o Purchase a binder ring (available at office and craft supply stores).
  - o In the corner of the photo card, using a hole puncher, make a hole and thread the photo cards through the binder ring.
  - o Make a cover page which indicates the year.
  - o Store in a photo safe box (acid and lignin free).

- **Add to an album.** Another option for photo cards is to trim them down to a standard 4x6 size and place them in a photo album or photo safe box.

- **Repurpose.** Traditional greeting cards can be cut and shaped to create gift tags which can be used for next year.

- **Share.** Trim your greeting cards leaving only the decorative side of the card and donate them to preschools, Girl Scout troops, nursing homes or churches who can make use of them in various craft projects.

130. I love after-Christmas sales! My goal is to buy gifts for next year, but I often make purchases with little thought about who I'm really buying for. Can you suggest a more organized plan?

Don't let your shopping savviness turn into next year's clutter. A planned shopping approach is all you need.

Before you venture out to the stores:

1. **Make a list.** Take an inventory of what you have from last years after-Christmas sale. Match up your current inventory with the recipients on your gift list.

2. **Shop.** This list will give you an idea of what gaps need to be filled. Stick with your list and purchase only what you need.

3. **Store**. Place all gift items in a labeled storage bin. Before closing up the bin, be sure to include your list of recipients and what their gift(s) will be.

4. **Check it twice.** Keep a copy of the list in a file labeled "Christmas" or take a photo and store in your smartphone. Before you go shopping again, be sure to check your list before buying anything — you may already have a gift waiting in your bin.

131. Do you have a foolproof approach to taking down and packing up Christmas decorations?

Cleaning up after the holidays is an ideal opportunity to rid yourself of clutter and decorations you no longer use.

When packing up your decorations, think first about how you prefer to decorate. If you enjoy decorations in the same place each year you may want to consider packing them up according to each room. Each storage box can be labeled and filled with all items for a specific room.

However, if you prefer to have a new view each year then group similar items together and pack them up in labeled bins.

No matter which way you decide to organize and store your decorations be mindful of your inventory along the way. If you did not use it, if something is broken or is no longer your style, donate those items rather than continue to provide storage for them. Keep your holiday trimmings current and it will make it easier to decorate and find what you need.

132. What suggestions do you have for keeping my Christmas lights from becoming a tangled mess?

You can preserve the longevity of your lights if they don't become a tangled mess every year. Wrap string lights around flat pieces of cardboard or a cardboard paper towel roll. Place them side by side in their own labeled storage bin and you'll never have to wrestle with your lights again.

This reminds me of a fun story, a couple of years ago, I let my kids create the photo for our family Christmas card. The girls took string lights and wrapped them around my son and put duct tape on his mouth. The caption read "Silent Night" and you can see the card on the ATO Pinterest board.

Simple is the new black.

&ev Sandra Lane &ev

Notes

1. Ray A. Smith, "A Closet Filled with Regrets," The Wall Street Journal, April 17, 2013, accessed March 2018, https://www.wsj.com/articles/SB10001424127887324240804578415002232186418.

2. P. D. Bliese, J. R. Edwards, and S. Sonnentag, "Stress and well-being at work: A century of empirical trends reflecting theoretical and societal influences," *Journal of Applied Psychology,* March 2017; *102*(3), 389-402, accessed March 2018 doi:10.1037/apl0000109.

3. S. McMains, and S. Kastner, "Interactions of Top-down and bottom-up mechanisms in human visual cortex," *Journal of Neuroscience*, January 2011, accessed March 2018, doi: 10.1523/JNEUROSCI.3766-10.2011

4. T. Amer, K. L. Campbell, and L. Hasher, "Cognitive control as a double-edged sword," *Trends in Cognitive Sciences,* 2016; *20*(12), 905-915, accessed January 2018, doi:10.1016/j.tics.2016.10.002.

5. L. R. Vartanian, K. M. Kernan, and B. Wansink, "Clutter, chaos, and overconsumption: The role of mind-set in stressful and chaotic food environments," *Environment and Behavior,* 2017; *49*(2), 215-223, accessed January 2018, doi:10.1177/0013916516628178.

6. M. S. Ponikowski, "Six Ways to help your Child Get a Good Night's Sleep," *Today's Parent,* November 2, 2017, accessed February 2018, https://www.todaysparent.com/kids/kids-sleep/.

7. Gloria Mark, *The Cost of Interrupted Work: More Speed and Stress*, accessed January 2018, https://www.ics.uci.edu/~gmark/chi08-mark.pdf.

8. Eric Clark, *The Real Toy Story: Inside the Ruthless Battle for America's Youngest Consumers* (New York: Free Press, 2007).

9. David Allen, *Getting Things Done* (New York: Penguin Books, 2001).

10. Brian Tracy, *Eat that Frog!* (Oakland: Berrett-Koehler Publishers, Inc, Second Edition, 2007).

11. Audrey Noble, "4 Ways to Be More Productive, According to Experts," TIME, September 25, 2018, accessed November 2018, http://time.com/5401177/how-to-be-more-productive-experts/.

12. "National Sleep Foundation Recommends New Sleep Times," February 2, 2015, accessed on July 2018, https://www.sleepfoundation.org/press-release/national-sleep-foundation-reommends-new-sleep-times.

13. S. Charron, E. Koechlin, "Divided Representation of Concurrent Goals in Human Frontal Lobes," *Science Magazine,* April 2010, accessed March 2018, doi:10.1126/science 118 3614.

14. "Junk Mail Reduction Kit," Center for Development of Recycling at San Jose State University, accessed March 2018, http://www.recyclestuff.org/media/ReducingJunkMailFinal.pdf.

15. "Being Perceived as a Hoarder May Cost Worker a Promotion, Finds New CareerBuilder Survey," CareerBuilder, accessed October 2018, http://press.careerbuilder.com/2011-08-03-Being-Perceived-as-a-Hoarder-May-Cost-Workers-a-Promotion-Finds-New-CareerBuilder-Survey.

16. "Study Results: The Effects of Digital Photo Organizing on American Families", 2016, accessed March 2018, https://everpresent.com/study-digital-photo-organizing-in-american-families/.

17. "Being Perceived as a Hoarder May Cost Worker a Promotion, Finds New CareerBuilder Survey," CareerBuilder, accessed October 2018, http://press.careerbuilder.com/2011-08-03-Being-Perceived-as-a-Hoarder-May-Cost-Workers-a-Promotion-Finds-New-CareerBuilder-Survey.

Acknowledgements

I am grateful to God for providing me with the skills to recognize procrastination, make lists, manage my time and projects. Without those skills, I would not have a business or a book.

My heartfelt appreciation goes to my family and friends for your encouragement and support. Especially, my husband, Greg and children, Sydney and Grant, who lift me up when needed and stay away from my closed office door when I was doing deep work. I give thanks to my sister in-law, Lila, who gave me a supportive nudge in the summer of 2010 when I was thinking of starting this business.

This book could not have been accomplished without the patience, guidance and reassurance from my book coach, Shawndra Holmberg, the creative artwork from my graphic designer, Kari Miller, the attention to detail from my manuscript readers, Roger and Pamela Wright and, of course, the questions from clients, acquaintances and strangers. Thank you!!

About the Author

Sandra Lane was born and raised in the Garden State of New Jersey. For the last 25 years, she happily calls Sewickley, PA home.

Sandra credits her early organizing interest to her parents. Dad was a skilled carpenter who kept a meticulous wood shop with every screw, nail and tool in its own special place. Mom was a planner, writing down lists to stay focused and meet objectives whether she was hosting a party or organizing a meeting.

Sandra started her business, Organization Lane, LLC, in 2010 as a hobby. However, it soon turned into a bona fide company that is more of a ministry as she sees the transformation that takes place with each client and feels blessed to partner with them through the process. In addition to hands-on organizing work with clients, she speaks to numerous groups each year on a variety of organizing topics.

Sandra is a Board Certified Professional Organizer. She is an active member of the National Association of Productivity and Organizing Professionals (NAPO) and has served as the Pittsburgh NAPO Chapter Membership Director, Vice-President and President. She is a member of the Institute for Challenging Disorganization (ICD).

Sandra is married with two children of her own, ages 22 and 19 and is the host mom for an exchange student from Venezuela, age 23.

In addition to running her business, she volunteers at her church and garden club, all of which tests her own organizational skills every day.

If you like this book, please don't keep it a secret. Tell your friends about it and write a review on Amazon. Thank you in advance.

Made in United States
Orlando, FL
02 September 2022

21907363R00076